# I Am the Product of Rape

# I Am the Product of Rape

## A Memoir

*Catherine Wyatt-Morley*

*Epilogue by Jalyon Welsh-Cole*

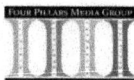

Four Pillars Media Group

Library of Congress Cataloging-in-Publication Data
Wyatt-Morley, Catherine
        I Am the Product of Rape—A Memoir/by Catherine Wyatt-Morley
ISBN 978-0-9966242-0-6
Library of Congress Control Number: 2018902535
Cover design by Angela Rosa Hurston
Editing by Steven Morley
Copyedit by Patricia Harmon

Printed in the United States of America on acid-free paper

Women On Maintaining Education and Nutrition
http://www.educatingwomen.org
http://www.CatherineWyatt-Morley.com

First Edition 2018

## || Dedication ||

This book is dedicated to overcoming all of yesterday's pain. May the winds of time blow you away and, in your place, may grace, safety, restoration, love and healing reside.

## ||Foreword||

What once started out as a typical day on the job launched a more than 20-year friendship and professional relationship with a woman who is self-described as the "Product of Rape." More than 20 years ago, at a first-person speaking engagement, I encountered a woman who was a tough-talking, brutally outspoken, health education operative. Intrigued by her story, I approached her with an encouraging and friendly comment. Quickly she rebuffed me and let me know that she did not require friends. Even then she was a determined warrior in life.

*I Am the Product of Rape—A Memoir* is written by the woman I met that day, Catherine Wyatt-Morley. This book tells the true story of an adopted girl, born on the dirt floor of a basement to a 12-year old mother. Catherine was fathered by a threatening, manipulative rapist in the midst of an incestuous family environment in Flint, Michigan.

The story of the lives of the members of these two families — one adoptive and one by birth — advances through the decades to expose deception. The truth of this four-generational memoir could only be told from the inside. I can attest to this author's fortitude and astonishing ability to absorb repeated emotional gut-punches introspectively as she shares her life honestly.

Unashamed to rely on the advice of a trusted mental health professional, Catherine sifts gingerly through the excruciatingly painful pieces of her shattered life. She opens the closed doors of her adoption process and takes a hard look at the tragic lives hidden in the filed-away interviews and documents. Finally, she shares the heart-wrenching truth that incest travelled past her generation to affect her children. Catherine writes the details of her life with transparency and laser insight. At times, this results in bone-chilling effects.

The story breaths the essence of truth that incest, rape and abuse often go unnoticed. Friends and family members in the same household remain quiet, harboring fear and embarrassment, unwilling to sound an alarm or speak out. Through sacrifice and sharing, Catherine leads by example, showing others with similar experiences what can and, most importantly, what must be done to reach a positive outcome.

*I Am the Product of Rape—A Memoir* was written to bring to light the negative effects of secrets and lies hidden beneath the shadows of shame and low self-esteem. In that light, former victims can take back their power, knowing that rape, incest and abuse can no longer prevent their breakthrough.

As a woman who has experienced sexual abuse as a child and rape as an adult, I choose to add my voice in support of Catherine's efforts to bring this subject to light. As an administrator of public housing services where more than 75% of the residents are women, I recognize that many have also experienced rape, incest or sexual violence at some point in their lives. I am eager to assist in obliterating the systems of denial, silence, secrecy, and darkness that prohibit safe, secure futures.

In the years since we met, through the hell, high water and celebrations of life, the woman who needed no friends and I have become true friends. When her first book was just a collection of letters to her children, I encouraged her to turn them into a book. Now completing this her fourth book, she has raised the children she once feared she would not see grow up. Point of fact, my dear friend has also crafted literature for medical journals. When life's circumstances called for Catherine to appoint someone to be prepared to stand in as a second mother to her children, I did so with fear and trembling.

Today, I am very proud to see that Catherine's daughter Jalyon — once a little girl sharing meals and making jewelry at my kitchen table — has made use of the power within her to encourage and uplift others.

In the latter part of this memoir, Jalyon describes her own experiences as the fourth generation affected by the interwoven intergenerational trauma. In print and in action, she is a fierce warrior in the fight for the lives of those who have experienced abuse, incest and rape.

My many thanks go to these two brave women for forging ahead, having the perseverance to spend years searching for the truth, the courage to look that truth squarely in the face, and the guts to declare that it can no longer have the power to silence their unified voice.

Karen Bowens
Resident Services Director
Fayetteville Metropolitan Housing Authority

## ||Preface||

To appreciate the importance of this book and why each of us should care, take a moment and envision a child that you love withstanding ongoing physical and emotional, torturous abuse. With each turn of the page, you will be immersed in a host of emotions, as your inner being begins to grasp the magnitude of secrets and the consequences of denial.

The reality of knowing that incest can happen to you, or someone you love, is unsettling. I had no idea that, by unveiling the sealed secrets of my past, I had also provided my daughter with the courage to embark upon her own unimaginable journey from hell to healing.

I recognize that this book will challenge you to think about your past, perhaps evoke some uncomfortable memories, and quite possibly create a great deal of controversy. However, I am confident it will increase public awareness, initiate discussion, promote healing and, in turn, make major change in the lives of our children, our loved ones, society as a whole and those most affected by the carnage left behind.

As this book came to its conclusion, and with the realization of my daughter's unwarranted pain, I take comfort in realizing that together our life's narrative includes advocating on behalf of victims of incest.

We are dedicated to raising awareness regarding this and its related subjects, which are most often overlooked, or from which most people easily disconnect themselves.

As my daughter and I take you through our journey, remember that we are committed to stopping the intergenerational trauma within our family and we are hopeful this memoir and our message helps to free you in some small way.

*Now is the time!*

Since the title of this book didn't stop you from picking it up, it's quite possible you already understand the subject matter involves such disturbing topics as incest, rape and sexual abuse. Let me first say thank you for your interest in reading my story and that of my daughter. We share our journey with the deep and sincere hope that it will open doors of healing and growth for anyone who has experienced sexual abuse, been connected to an abusive family system, felt the wrath of rejection, or walked the often jagged pathways of foster care and adoption.

For the emotional and psychological well-being of all who hold this book in their hands, however, I would caution that some of the material in this book is graphic in its description and uncompromising in its depiction of the wickedness and cruelty common to sexual abusers and the weakness and deception common to those manipulated into cooperating with them. Nevertheless, there is much more to this book than graphic details of acts from which many would prefer to cover their eyes.

Also involved in this multi-generational family history of incest and rape is the story of my journey through foster homes and adoption, and the intense emotional peaks and valleys that I experienced while searching for and locating, my biological mother and family of origin. All of this information has been shared with the intention of leading others toward the healing I have found in the process of dealing with my personal challenges and the family atrocities I eventually learned had taken place.

Reading this book could, in some instances, result in extreme emotional responses, triggering levels of distress for which certain readers may be unprepared. It is highly common for victims of childhood sexual abuse to have no conscious memories of abusive episodes. Being exposed to information about such encounters has the potential to release repressed memories.

If you suspect that you may be a victim of unremembered childhood sexual abuse (resources listed at back of book), please be sure you have a trusted counselor, pastor or other professional ready to assist you in the case of traumatic reactions. At the very least, please be sure you have a supportive friend or group of friends able to listen to your concerns about this very uncomfortable and culturally controversial topic.

If you read no further than this page, please choose to believe that you have vast value as a created human being and that abuse, whether sexual, emotional, physical, or in some other form, is an inexcusable evil. If you know, or should come to remember, that such abuse or violation has happened to you, reject the abuse and any negative messages it has tried to speak toward you. Reject the abuse, but *embrace yourself.* Victims deserve compassion, a chance to tell their own story, and the peace of mind that comes from knowing — whether or not they can accept this truth at the present time — that they're worthy, unique individuals with dignity and a purpose on the planet.

I can personally testify that there is a purpose in all that I've been through. The events described in *I am the Product of Rape—A Memoir* led me to the great privilege of reaching out to others with a story in which, somehow, horror becomes hope.

## ||Introduction||

*A ferocious human predator ripped through our family,
drooling over the innocent—leaving none untouched.*

In the process of writing this book, an extremely
difficult journey that has taken years, I was taken to
unfamiliar destinations and exposed to unfathomable pain.
Part of that pain was learning that I was created through
the atrocities of incest by a brutally manipulative monster
and, while only moments old, denied by a heartless
grandmother who never bothered to look at me.

Another difficult truth is that I was carried in the
belly of an immature, vulnerable child, connected by the
lifeline that carried the blood-rich oxygen and nutrients
from her to me, only to be rejected by her from my first
breath.

My intention for this book is to provide insight into
the consequences of family secrets, conspiracy, lies, and
denial. Told from my perspective, this is my family story, a
snapshot of four women irreversibly scarred by traumatic
abuse.

First, the family matriarch, a prolific mother of ten,
sets the tone for the women who would place their feet in
the footprints of her journey, transforming her ancestry for
generations to come. Her story sheds light on the
transgressions she not only allowed but participated in.

Next, there is the girl who endured the death of her childhood at the hands of incest, abuse, betrayal, humiliation, rape, and the inevitable birth of a child. Well before puberty she was sexually exploited in her own home, her childhood, mind and body all repeatedly violated.

Then, there is me. *I Am the Product of Rape—A Memoir.* I am an adoptee, I am a daughter, and I am a mother of three. In search of my future, I found the weighted baggage of the past. Catholic Social Services documents helped to chronicle my life, as did the many conversations I have had over the years with sometimes very reluctant people—relatives, social workers, and paper pushers, all of whom seemed to guard my past as it floundered aimlessly, leaving lingering, unanswered questions.

I found and met my mother well into my adulthood, listening intently as she exposed the atrocities which resulted in my birth. She transmitted the pain of a denied childhood to me like so many nutrients fed to a fetus through an umbilical cord. My heritage lay bare; I was speechless as my mother's portrait of her sexual violation crushed me. I was faced with her reality, my subsequent reality, and with what was yet to come.

Finally, along this sexual-abuse sojourn, I unfortunately discovered my daughter's devastating experience. Crushing my very core, this revelation sent my life careening in another unexpected direction, straight through my children's lives into a fourth-generation nightmare.

The ripple effects of demoralizing incest, the sexual slavery of serial rape, and the brutality of molestation go beyond their impact on the direct victims, transmitting a trauma that oozes intergenerationally. This story intertwines the DNA of my family's bloodline.

## ||Kept Secrets||

In sharing this book's content, women and girls began coming forward and sharing their experiences, commending me for the courage to discuss these taboo subjects and confirming the great need for this memoir. Two hundred and fifty women from around the country participated in a short anonymous survey, conducted over a six-month period during the crafting of this memoir.

I quickly discovered that 98% of respondents knew someone (friend or relative) who had been raped; 96% had been raped; 50% had unreported exposure of incest during childhood by a family member; 80% had not received mental health services but were willing to receive mental health services if their confidentiality would be maintained; 100% never reported incest, molestation or sexual assault to authorities; 40% were raped in marriage by their spouses; 100% had or have feelings of guilt and self-blame; 85% struggle in personal relationships; 20% were mothers of a child who raped his own sister and never sought help for the children nor themselves.

As women relieved themselves of secrets long hidden behind mother-daughter relationships that were not so warm and fuzzy — involving life-altering experiences with secret adoption or forced abortions and life-transforming journeys through a foster care system that was not always kind—I recognized that my family was not alone in its experiences.

In coffee shop discussions, at restaurants, through emails, and during airplane conversations, I found incest, rape, and molestation to be shrouded in secrecy and buried in the psyches of many women.

Women were often interested in discussions, though almost always those discussions would be on behalf of "a friend." Instinctively, in many cases, I believe some of these vulnerable victims were uncomfortable or unwilling to reveal their stories firsthand, owing to the shame, stigma, heaviness or guilt that make them reluctant to bring such ugliness to light. Often overlooked, excused, and even denied, abuse takes on infinite forms — this is especially true of psychological abuse.

*You are not alone!*

# Table of Contents

## The Good Wife

*B*orn in Chicago in 1926, Tawana Jo was twenty years old and living in Louisville, Kentucky, when she gave birth to her first daughter, Angela, in 1946. Her second, Violet, was born in 1948. Both daughters were born during her marriage to a man named Allen Blackmore, a marriage that soon dissolved in divorce. Desiring to put distance between them, she took her two young daughters to Flint, Michigan, in 1951. Living in a small tenement apartment, Tawana Jo struggled to put food on the table for herself and her girls. She worked at the Montgomery Ward department store in downtown Flint, but her job did not pay much and opportunities for a young, single black mother were not plentiful. She needed every dime until she could find a better job, and she worked diligently, hoping to advance.

Within months of relocating, she met thirty-three-year-old Broderick, a shrewd, smooth-talking man who approached everything he did with intent. Broderick spotted her working in the men's department of Montgomery Ward, arranging a display of dress shirts on the main aisle of the store. She wore a dress that was years old but nonetheless very flattering, showing off her slender waist. The neckline was modest, revealing just enough to pique his interest. His attention, however, only fleetingly lingered on her attractive physique. One quick glance confirmed that her ring finger was bare. He could tell from the slightly faded color of the fabric that the dress was probably one of a few and had been worn many times. If she was lacking in personal possessions, he reckoned, she may well have other financial responsibilities. Children, perhaps? Narrowing his eyes, he watched as she stacked each shirt very deliberately, neatly arranging each by size and color. She was very careful with details, he noted—a characteristic that suggested she wasn't a carefree single woman, but more likely a young mother.

Absorbed in her work, she gradually became aware of a man watching her from a few aisles away. She noticed his stylish haircut and, even from a distance, she could tell he was well dressed. As he slowly, methodically ambled in her direction, she noticed the gleam of his finely polished shoes. Tawana Jo pretended not to notice as he worked his way over to her.

"Excuse me," he said, as he approached, "Can you tell me where to find the dress socks? I'm looking for cream-colored ones to match a suit."

Eagerly, Tawana Jo said, "I can show you better than I can tell you. Follow me, sir—this way." Following closely behind, he noticed the deliberate swing of her hips. As they neared the men's hosiery aisle, Broderick strode in front of her, no longer in need of her assistance. Tawana Jo was mesmerized by his swagger and the alluring scent of his cologne. It was a heavy, masculine scent, one she did not recognize. This increased her curiosity about this man, a black man with confidence and, apparently, no shortage of funds. His fragrance lingered long after he had thanked her courteously and she walked away to resume her stocking tasks.

Later that evening, as her shift was ending, she saw him standing near the door, evidently waiting for her. She did her best to act completely surprised. Looking straight at her with a captivating smile, Broderick said, "I couldn't stop thinking about you, so I had to come back and ask . . . would you allow me to walk you to the bus stop?"

Flattered but not wanting to seem overly eager, Tawana Jo coyly said, "Well . . . I just might let you do that." Broderick inquired if she was in a hurry to get home. "Well," she answered, "my daughters are waiting to be picked up and fed, so I don't really have a choice about that!" She worried to herself that this information might dampen his interest in her. To her relief, he showed particular attention to her comment about motherhood, seeming to find this fact to his liking.

Initially conducting himself as the perfect gentleman, Broderick began courting Tawana Jo, finding her two young girls to be very pretty and well-behaved. Their short courtship was filled with long walks, family picnics and girl play as she learned of Broderick's upbringing in New Iberia, Louisiana. The fourth of twelve children, he spoke of dropping out of school after completing the sixth grade, the chaos and enjoyable excitement of such a large family and his mother's gentle care for her large family. He boasted about his honorable discharge from the military but was reluctant to discuss his first marriage, which had produced a son. In time, Tawana Jo was able to get him to tell her all about his only son, James, who lived with his mother in New York.

Broderick's strong religious beliefs and Roman Catholic heritage intrigued her, as she had not previously believed attending church was relevant to her life. However, since Broderick attended Mass every Sunday without exception, Tawana Jo saw to it that she and her children attended church regularly. He soon made himself a fixture at Tawana Jo's small tenement apartment. She was impressed by his first-rate carpentry skills and captivated by his ability to draw complex diagrams and bring them to life. He built beds for the children and became her personal handyman.

Tawana Jo was very attracted to his short, muscular build. Just the scent of him as he walked into the room sparked her imagination as his caramel complexion, clear, deep brown eyes and beautiful jet-black hair stirred something in her that she had not felt with her first husband. When he spoke slowly to her in his exotic French Creole accent, the radiating smile that spread across his face, lighting up his eyes, seemed to whisper romance to her.

She willingly gave herself to him, believing in their love. Nothing would get in the way of making him her man. Imagining herself as Mrs. Broderick Freeman, she was consumed by thoughts of making love to him, having his children, keeping his home, and becoming the center of his universe. His maturity, self-confidence, practical skills and dependable General Motors job were also welcome assets to Tawana Jo, who longed for more—far more—than the just-enough she had.

After marrying in Toledo, Ohio, in 1951, Tawana Jo and Broderick moved their family into a small home on the south side of Flint. They began building an admirable Catholic home, the kind that most Negroes of the time aspired to have. A stay-at-home mother, Tawana Jo took pride in keeping her children neat and clean, keeping her home in order, and making sure to look beautiful and be ready for her husband when he came home from work. She wanted things to be perfect for him.

She reverenced him, believing he was her and her children's saving grace. Newlywed Broderick became the picture-perfect husband to his young bride, flattering her and carefully praising her domestic and maternal skills. Seemingly taking to fatherhood, he consistently complimented her well-mannered girls and read stories to them, always obliging their requests for just one more. Violet, the younger one, had taken to him instantly, but Broderick took special interest in Angela, the bashful, reserved oldest. It would take a while, he realized, to gain her trust. From the outside the Freeman household appeared wonderfully strong. Inside, though, something insidious was silently growing.

## Time to Begin

*B*y the end of 1953, Tawana Jo had conceived three children in quick succession, making her a busy mother of five. Relieved that she had found such a responsible father and friend, she was living blissfully in a financial paradise. Whatever she desired, her husband seemed pleased to supply. Their children's needs were always met. As head of the Freeman household, nothing was out of reach for his growing family.

Broderick's charming personality had won him the admiration of his church family and co-workers, who respected his skills and tireless work ethic. When he wasn't at work, busy on his side carpentry projects or lending a hand at the church he held dear, he consistently helped out with his two stepdaughters, always showing particular attention to Angela. Though she remained reserved, over time she began to relax around her stepfather. His attention to her gave him the appearance of being a doting parent; in reality, the pedophile lurking within him patiently studied the child. He assessed his position in her life, gave his time to her, and worked to gain her trust with the intention of betraying it and eventually having her. Using his keen, predatory instincts, Broderick schooled himself regarding Angela's mental and emotional strengths and vulnerabilities. While sizing her up carefully over a span of many months, he attempted to satisfy his ravenous sexual hunger on his wife, concealing his perverted desires by fathering child after child.

Seven-year-old Angela began to believe her father seemed to genuinely care about her and the things her childish mind would create. He listened intently as she would go on and on about her dolls, school, clothes and games, often praising her for being such a good little girl or being supportive whenever she complained about chores or problems with her friends, even her mother. He was particularly interested in her interactions with her friends and the other adults in her life. He methodically kept tabs on his older stepdaughter, aiming to direct her affections and trust away from anyone other than himself. It was his way of guarding what he privately had begun to think of as his personal territory.

Unbeknownst to her, Angela was falling victim to her daddy's superficial interest in her relationships outside the home and her immediate family, which felt to her like benevolent concern for her well-being. Her pure, youthful love came wrapped in what would become complete trust. She began to enjoy their time together, innocently welcoming his shoulder rubs, kisses and hugs, and even returning his gentle affection.

Feeling sick one morning, Tawana Jo made a doctor's appointment for the following afternoon. When she mentioned it to Broderick, he immediately offered to stay home from work with the three small children and get snacks for the older two when they came home from school. Gratified at feeling like the selfless savior to his family, his mind silently spun with possibilities. Arriving home from school the next day, Angela and Violet sat down with their siblings to a peanut butter and jelly sandwich. Broderick asked them about school and homework, and both girls were eager to tell all of the day's events.

Eyeing Angela's ease and enthusiasm around him, he told her he had a special gift for her because she was doing so well in school. A smile spread across her face as she asked, "What is it?" she asked excitedly. "Where is it?"

"You'll see," he said.

"Daddy, what about *me*?" pleaded Violet, her face wrinkling in disappointment.

"Not today, baby, but if you do a good job on your homework, maybe Daddy will think of something you'll like," he said. Firmly, he added, "Today is just for Angela. Do you understand?"

Feeling frightened by his harsh tone, Violet looked down at the tile floor and softly said, "Yes, Daddy."

After they'd finished their snack, Broderick put the three little ones down to nap and told Violet to go into her room, mollifying her with a reminder that a good job on her homework might mean a treat for her later. Turning to Angela, who seemed almost unable to contain herself, he told her to look for her surprise down in the basement. As she enthusiastically searched, she could hear Broderick's deliberate footsteps coming down the basement stairs. "Where *is* it?" she begged.

Approaching her, he put his hand on her shoulder and pointed to the furthest corner of the basement. His touch seemed rougher than usual to Angela, but it was only a fleeting sensation that quickly passed as she innocently rushed in the direction her father had indicated. The dim light and dank odor there suddenly felt scary, and she paused for an instant. In the disorienting half-light, her father suddenly looked like some kind of ferocious animal. Glancing up into his eyes for reassurance, she glimpsed something she could not identify. Gripped by terror, she came face to face with the essence of evil. Having waited long enough, her stepfather unleashed his desires and allowed them full expression.

Her breath caught in her throat as she felt hands violently pulling down her tights. With a thud, her small body hit the cement floor as he quickly knelt down between her unwilling, spread-apart legs. Stunned by the impact, she lay on the floor limply as fingers feverishly pulled at the buttons of her frilly blouse. Except for the awareness of her heart beating furiously in her chest, her thoughts muddled into a blur, unable to help her comprehend why her father was pressing himself against her, his breath coming out in hoarse gasps.

"Daddy, *NO, please,* don't!" she exclaimed in a harrowing, half-choked scream, as though desperately crying out to be rescued from this man who somehow looked like her stepfather but was a complete stranger to her. Pleading she cried, 'Daddy, *STOP, STOP, Daddy, NO, STOP!*' She felt hands clutch at her legs as her adrenaline surged, demanding that she wriggle free from this man's grasp. Leaning into her ear, as if someone might overhear, he menacingly whispered, "Don't say a word."

Tears stung her eyes as she felt his grasp intensify and heard a thin, metallic hissing sound she knew had been his zipper opening. With one hand he held her down as she tried in vain to escape his grip. She felt fabric chafing her tiny waist and upper thigh as the center of her panties were pulled roughly to one side. A rush of shame unjustly engulfed her heart as she felt his fingers probing their way inside her. Screams filled the air as she begged him '*STOP, STOP,* NO!'

Her body quivered as waves of fear washed over her. His erratic savagery met her bewildered stare. Squirming frantically and kicking under his heaving weight only seemed to increase the intensity of his movements, and a cold chill raced across her spine as she heard the frightening sound of moaning from deep in his throat. Spreading her tiny legs further apart, he brutally entered her. Her voice rose in an urgent cry. "*Don't!* It hurts, *it hurts!*" Waves of terror and confusion stole her ability to speak as he began grinding rhythmically, harder and harder, deep and deeper.

Her seven-year-old body was powerless as a blunt pressure and an excruciating burning feeling just below her tiny stomach forced out sounds she'd never uttered, in tandem with a piercing pain that penetrated her entire midsection. She felt her head jerk backwards and her chin thrust forward, and blood trickled from a corner of her mouth, where her teeth had caught the tip of her tongue.

Perspiration dripped from her forehead, mingling with her tears as she felt herself being pounded again and again against the damp, hard floor. Lacerating her hymen, he began verbally abusing her as his words cut as deep as his invasion. Able to neither endure nor escape the grinding pressure that locked her small frame to his against every shred of her will, she allowed her mind to float mercifully outside herself, fixing her gaze on a spreading splotch of mildew on the ceiling. Noticing the musty odors of the moisture-stained walls just behind her head, she closed her eyes.

Deep sounds seemed to be coming from within his chest, and a sudden torrent of angry, cutting words again spilled from his core. Glaring down at her with a psychotic, crazed look in his eyes, Angela was jarred back to consciousness as he threw his head back, unleashing sexed-up baritone utterances, violently thrashing his body against hers. Feeling the fullness of his weight suddenly collapsing on top of her in completion, she became sickened by the smell of his breath.

Quickly regaining control, Broderick stood up, looked down at her small body and smiled. Pointing to the opposite corner of the basement, he loudly demanded she take off her panties, put them in the dirty laundry pile and go upstairs to her room. Petrified, stumbling to her feet, she did as she was told. Sobbing, she walked toward the laundry pile. "Shut up!" he snapped. Quietly, and in excruciating pain both physical and emotional, Angela walked slowly upstairs, Broderick close behind her.

Once in her room, Angela climbed onto her bed and curled up into a ball, crying as though her very heart was crumbling. Panic again gripped her as her bedroom door burst open. Broderick entered her room, and walked over to her bed as she laid there quivering. He leaned over, kissed her forehead, and said, "Tell no one." He turned and walked out. She crawled out of her bed and crowded herself into her closet.

Wrapping herself into a tight ball in her lightless closet, she sat in stillness as dull pain continued to radiate through the middle of her body. The physical damage, as awful as it felt, would pale in comparison to the lingering wreckage inflicted upon her self-image. Her knight-in-shining-armor daddy, without any reason a seven-year-old child could possibly comprehend, had committed a dehumanizing act against her, sending a chill through her that settled deep into her soul.

Every affectionate touch, every kind word, every act of fatherly care she believed she had experienced were now nullified by his egregiously evil attack and the callousness he now showed toward her. Unable to make sense of what he had done to her, her mind began discarding the many memories of times when he told her what a good, well-behaved little girl she was. For the rest of the evening she stayed in her bedroom sobbing quietly until she had no more tears, emotionally shocked and traumatized by her father's irreparable brutality. No one, including her mother, checked on her.

The next morning Angela sat silently at the breakfast table. Violet happily chattered about schoolmates and what she planned to have for lunch. Tawana Jo asked Angela, "Are you feeling all right?" Angela said nothing. After getting the two older children off to school, as the younger ones watched TV, Tawana Jo gathered the children's clothes for washing. She felt a wave of nausea as she stood looking at Angela's bloodstained panties, marked by what looked like stiffened drops of dried semen. Immediately her motherly instincts told her what had happened to her daughter. Shocked and incensed, her thoughts suddenly turned to herself. How was she going to tell her husband she was pregnant again with baby number six?

That afternoon, when Broderick came home from work, she calmly confronted him. She told him she had found the panties, attempting to hand them to him.

"What did you do to Angela while I was at the doctor?"
Instantly he became defensive, flatly denied any
wrongdoing, and walked out of the room. His reaction
mystified her. Standing with the dirty clothes around her
feet, a flurry of thoughts flooded her mind. *Where
would she go? Who would care for her?* As she held her
stomach, she considered her situation. *I'm pregnant. I
cannot afford to leave. I haven't even told him about the
baby.* Then she reasoned to herself, *it was just one time.
He'll change. If I keep myself up, do everything I can to
please him, give myself to him more often, he'll only
want me. I can save our marriage.* She loved her life. She
loved him. Somehow, she felt she could trust the man
her own daughter could never trust again.

At that moment, Tawana Jo made a decision that
would have a domino effect on her life, Angela's life and
the lives of future generations who would become
genetically tied to incest, rape and abuse, directly and
indirectly. She would stay! Starting soon thereafter, back
to back, came babies number seven, eight, nine and ten.

Over the next five years Broderick solidified into
a consistently cold-blooded, heat-seeking animal,
dehumanizing Angela whenever he chose, asserting his
superiority. Aggressive and mean, Broderick became
more and more domineering as the years went on. No
one protected Angela. No one rescued her. Her mother,
using the power of denial to disconnect from Angela,
became increasingly unresponsive to her needs. Tawana
Jo did nothing to stop her husband's gut-wrenching

exploitation, denying the incest and sexual torture of her young daughter.

Sacrificing her daughter as payment for the comfort of a stable home and lifestyle, she allowed her narcissistic husband to unearth his perverted sexual hunger, which he frequently unleashed on her vulnerable child. It knew no satisfaction; in fact, getting away with abusing Angela fed his sense of personal power, which perpetuated the sickening cycle of sexual abuse and domination.

The moment Tawana Jo entered the door of denial, she began making it her life's work. With a practiced smile, she helped her husband hide the monster within, allowing her daughter to endure his savagery. In that, she was complicit. Together she and her husband presented a united front as upstanding, active, Catholic parishioners sitting front and center with their family every Sunday for Mass—after which he would fondle, grope, forcibly violate and otherwise repeatedly molest his stepdaughter. Unexplainably, Broderick's sincere and apparently committed love of the cross did little to diminish his pedophilic appetite, and Angela's mother did nothing. Tawana Jo was *the good wife.*

## Basement Birth

*I*t was still pitch-black outside Angela's window when she stumbled out of bed as quickly as she could, ran to the bathroom and threw up. Taking care not to wake anyone, she tiptoed back to her room when nausea overcame her again. Gagging, she again dashed toward the bathroom as a spasm sent vomit across the floor, missing the toilet altogether. Mopping up the mess with a towel as best she could in her weakened condition, she again eased back into her room but the pain radiating across her stomach made sleep elusive for what seemed like hours.

Lying awake in the darkness, Angela tried to find explanations for the changes in her body that were making her feel scared. She thought back to the day when she started her period the year prior. She had begun to bleed into her panties, and she had stomach cramps and felt slightly sick. She nervously told her mother. Together they went to the store and bought a sanitary belt and a package of sanitary napkins. Angela remembered being embarrassed as her mother talked to her about menstruation and the right way to put on the belt and hook the pad between her legs so her panties wouldn't get blood on them.

As she lay in the silent darkness with her eyes closed and both hands over her mouth, fighting off involuntary urges to vomit, it occurred to her that it had been months since she menstruated. But this was a different kind of sick feeling. Her head began to spin and she felt what seemed like movement inside her belly. But she had to be mistaken, she thought. *Is there something wrong with me? Am I dying?*, she wondered.

Exhausted, she drifted back into a restless sleep, a welcome escape from the instinctual yet unexplainable fear mounting within her, even if it wasn't peaceful sleep.

Purse in hand, her mother walked briskly into her room. "Angela, it's eight o'clock. Get up. Me and your dad have something to do this morning. I will need you to get the children's breakfast and make sure they're dressed. Mop the kitchen floor, scrub the bathtub and toilet, and clean up the bedrooms. We'll be gone for a while." Tawana Jo's voice echoed in Angela's spinning head. "Girl, did you hear me? I said get up!"

"Momma, I don't feel good," came Angela's muffled voice. Rolling over towards the door, she said, "Momma?" Tawana Jo had already left her room.

It was Saturday, August 30, 1958. Forcing herself to sit up on the side of the bed, feeling drained, dizzy, and sick to her stomach, she remembered having had stomach cramps and some kind of shooting back pain the night before. Left at home to care for her eight sisters and brothers, Angela forced herself to put her nausea and cramping aside as she prepared breakfast, washed dishes, cleaned the bathroom, got everyone bathed, teeth brushed, beds made and hair combed.

Ignoring her body, her mind wandered through the list of chores she had yet to do. It was 12:30. Exhausted, she just wanted to sit down. But there was more to do. Holding her stomach, she worked her way to the top of the basement stairs. Switching on the light, she began searching the long, dark stairwell for the bucket and mop she needed to clean the kitchen floor. As with most basements in Flint, over the years they became a place of storage, harboring moisture through the leaky walls.

Bedding, sofas, and fabrics would absorb foul odors, begin to decay, and host the stench. Small cracks developed over the rough, unfinished wall surfaces, while, over time, mold grew and the odor increased. Owing to the long, brutal winters, heat from the furnace and abundant spring rains, the basement walls had expanded and contracted, giving way to even more sources of moisture, decay and funky smells.

However, beyond all this, this basement held a much deeper wound for Angela. She saved her mopping chore for last because she abhorred the basement. Standing at the top of the stairs, her heart sank as her thoughts went back to that first instance of brutality. Bringing her thoughts back into focus and taking a deep breath, she braced herself, grabbing the handrail as she worked her way carefully down the steps. Midway down, a shock wave consumed her. Stumbling to the bottom stair, she cast a long, slim shadow amidst the dimly lit subterranean room. The dark basement corners haunted her, but she had to get the bucket. Cautiously, Angela crept to the edge of the pooled light where the bucket waited. Reaching for it, she suddenly felt water running down her legs, pooling at her feet.

Stunned, trying to understand what was happening to her, she stood frozen until a shriek of pain escaped her lips. A sharp pain wrapped around her from her lower back to the front of her pelvis, squeezing her so tightly she thought she would faint. Breathless and sweating, her knees buckled beneath her. As she sank to the floor, desperately she wanted the unwelcome intrusion to pass.

As she recovered from one searing pain, another would follow, racking her body in waves. Again, and again the pain came with greater force and frequency. Her attempts to get up from the filthy basement floor ended in a ripping pain that caused her to cry out in fear.

Momentarily, the pain subsided long enough for her to hear Violet and Percella making their way down the stairs, bellowing her name. "Angela! Angela! Are you okay? We're scared! Where are you? Come get us." As Angela opened her mouth to answer them, a bloodcurdling yell escaped her lips as another burning pain overtook her. She whispered to herself, "I'm scared, too." Quietly she managed to say, "What is *happening* to me?"

At the bottom of the stairs, Violet and Percella moved towards Angela, finding her lying in what appeared to be a small puddle of bloody water. "Angela, what's this? Are you bleeding? Did you fall down? What's wrong?"

Unable to speak, gasping for air, Angela crawled in excruciating pain away from the puddle beneath her to the far corner of the stench-filled basement. With no prenatal care, childbirth classes, early- or late-stage pregnancy training, pre-labor or early labor breathing techniques, a twelve-year-old-girl—totally unaware of what was happening to her body—was in active labor in a dark, dingy basement.

Alone, afraid and exhausted, Angela finally surrendered to the contractions, breathing in mold and mildew. The stagnant basement odors made her labor all the worse, as she tried to restrict her breathing.

Screams tore through her. Tears and terror filled the basement as her siblings gathered around her asking, "What's wrong?" As the pain increased, she cried out to them to go down the street and get Mrs. Brown.

"Okay, okay, we'll be right back. Don't worry!" Running as fast as they could, her siblings scrambled to Mrs. Brown's house.

While her siblings stood at Mrs. Brown's front door hurriedly explaining their sister was lying on the basement floor in pain, Angela began to respond to her body's natural urges, despite having no conscious understanding of what was taking place. Removing her underwear, she held her breath and began to push. Pressing herself up on her elbows, her hands on the cold damp cement floor beside herself, she pushed again, and again.

With one final push, Angela was alone with her daughter.

*Her daughter . . .Me.*

In the ominous basement, I was born in panic and terror amid rodents, insects, spiders, cobwebs, bacteria, fungus, and rotting wood. Shortly thereafter, in came Mrs. Brown, a nurse by trade, following close behind the children through the dimly-lit basement. As Mrs. Brown approached and observed Angela lying on the dirty basement floor, she quickly assessed the situation. However improbable it was, she had clearly just given birth. Immediately, Mrs. Brown turned to the other children and told them to go upstairs. With her on the floor was my tiny, squirming body, lying on the bloody, dirty basement floor between Angela's legs, umbilical cord still attached.

Mrs. Brown spoke softly and compassionately, attempting to reassure Angela while she screamed in agony, as afterbirth oozed out of her onto the floor beside me. As I cried, Mrs. Brown picked me up. Leaning toward Angela, in a low voice, Mrs. Brown asked if she would like to hold her newborn daughter — *me.* Turning her head away from what seemed an awful sight, Angela whispered a barely audible "no."

Instructing Violet to bring her a sharp knife from the kitchen, Mrs. Brown cut the umbilical cord. "Take the children upstairs, Violet," Mrs. Brown said firmly. Ushering the children upstairs, Violet turned, saying, "Mrs. Brown, they're very worried about Angela."

"I know," Mrs. Brown said. Grabbing old rags, towels, shirts, anything she could find, Mrs. Brown began wiping up the bloody mess. Then she moved Angela's body slightly away from the blood, placing a sofa cushion under her head. Angela watched me crying softly as Mrs. Brown cleaned me with one of Broderick's old shirts. Turning to Violet, Mrs. Brown calmly told her to go upstairs and call for help. Violet nervously questioned, "What's, what's wrong with Angela?" Reassuringly, Mrs. Brown responded, "Everything's okay. Your sister's going to be okay. I just need you to be a big girl and go upstairs and call the operator. Tell her you need an ambulance sent to this address."

"Yes, ma'am." It was about four-thirty in the afternoon when Violet made the call.

Angela lay quietly, motionless. Waiting for help to arrive, the children gathered silently looking on as their sister lay on the floor of their family basement.

Recognizing Angela's uncomfortable state and her siblings' questioning stares, Mrs. Brown instructed the children to go outside and wait for the ambulance. Covering Angela in an old blanket, Mrs. Brown placed me, still wrapped in Broderick's old shirt, on the musty sofa nearby. The ambulance arrived. The paramedics followed the children to the basement, where Mrs. Brown was holding Angela's hand as she lay on the floor. Mrs. Brown informed the paramedics of what she found as they began assessing Angela's condition. Turning to me, the paramedic assessed my condition and informed Mrs. Brown that they would be taking Angela and me to St. Joseph Hospital.

Placing Angela on a stretcher, strapping her down, they took her up the stairs and out the front door. The neighbors were outside murmuring and looking intently at the Freemans' home. One of the paramedics could be heard saying, "She looks so young." I was carried from the basement by Mrs. Brown. At the top of the stairs the paramedic took me from Mrs. Brown's arms and placed me beside Angela.

Shortly thereafter, Angela's parents arrived home, where they were met with urgent news from their panic-stricken children. Mrs. Brown told them their daughter had given birth in the basement, and an ambulance had taken both her and the baby to St. Joseph Hospital. Mrs. Brown assured the Freemans that Angela and her baby were fine.

Upon arriving at the hospital, Mr. and Mrs. Freeman entered the emergency doors, met by Sister

Teresa, St. Joseph Hospital's Catholic Charities representative. She assured them their daughter and her baby had arrived safely and was being attended to. Sister Teresa asked to speak to the Freemans briefly before being taken to Angela's room. Hesitantly, they agreed and were taken to a small alcove a few feet away from Angela's room.

Sister Teresa began asking how Angela's pregnancy had progressed, and if she had any allergies. But before any more questions could be asked, Broderick interrupted, "We didn't know she was pregnant." Sister Teresa said, "Oh, I'm so sorry, this must be a shock."

"Yes it is," Mrs. Freeman said.

"We want to see her, now!" Broderick demanded. "What room is she in?"

"She's right here. I'll show you", Sister Teresa replied. Stunned by their claims of ignorance, Sister Teresa would later report in her written statement that "this seems almost unbelievable."

Tawana Jo and Broderick entered Angela's room with expressions of disgust as Angela returned their looks with tears. "Momma, I was so scared. I didn't know what was happening to me." Standing at the foot of her daughter's bed and trying to summon an expression of compassion, Tawana Jo stiffly patted her foot. Glaring at her, she managed a few words. "Shhhh, get some rest, Angela. We'll be back in the morning."

Firmly, almost menacingly, Broderick looked at Angela and said, "Don't talk to anybody." After a quick, pointed look at his wife as if to say "we're done here," he turned and left the room.

At that instant, as Angela lay staring into what she saw as her mother's hijacked soul, an unspoken something passed between them. As she removed her hand from atop her daughter's foot, the last fragile strands of their mother-daughter bond snapped. At the same moment Angela's heart shattered under the weight of unimaginable betrayal, Tawana Jo's own heart shut tight, no longer able to span the distance between motherly love and wifely obedience to a perverse and powerful man. Her decision was now final. "We'll be back in the morning." Tawana Jo turned and joined her husband in the hospital hallway. They drove home in silence. In the emptiness of her room, Angela sobbed until sleep finally, mercifully, came to her aid.

On the next day, Sunday, August 31, Angela awoke only to resume the nightmare of the previous evening. Broderick, with his wife by his side, entered Angela's room early the following morning and moved quickly towards Angela. Masterfully using his manipulation skills, he began brainwashing his victim once again. "Angela, your mother and I have spoken with Catholic Charities and they are going to arrange for an adoption. You must keep your mouth shut. Imagine what the church would think of what you have done. You must keep your mouth shut, you hear me? Her face reddening, she sheepishly responded, "Yes, sir."

Shortly thereafter, Sister Teresa came to Angela's room to find her in bed flanked by her parents. As she entered, an intense conversation between the three of them stopped abruptly.

"Hello, Angela, I am Sister Teresa. I am with Catholic Charities. I stopped by to talk to you. Is that okay?"

"Yes, ma'am."

Mr. and Mrs. Freeman moved to one side as she approached Angela's bedside. "Angela, I need to discuss what happened. We need to talk about the baby." Sister Teresa asked Angela how she felt. Angela looked away. Sister asked Angela her age. Angela said nothing. "Do you need a pillow? Can I get you anything?" Angela said nothing. Sister asked if she was hungry. Again, Angela spoke not a word. Sister turned to Mr. and Mrs. Freeman, "Is Angela okay? Has she discussed anything with you?" Mrs. Freeman, looking at Angela, said, "Yes, she's fine, just tired."

Turning toward Angela, Sister could see she was not interested in—or perhaps did not feel safe—discussing anything. "Okay, I am sure you are tired. You have had a lot happen." Sister realized she was not going to get her to talk. "I will come back to speak with you later." As Sister turned to leave she asked Mrs. Freeman softly, "Has she told you who the alleged father is?"

"No, she has not."

"Will you please step into the hall for a moment?" She asked the Freemans if Angela had spoken to them about the baby. They said she had not. The Freemans informed Sister that they would like to have "it" placed in an adoption facility as soon as possible.

"Are you sure? Don't you want more time to think this over?" Sister asked. "Have you discussed this with Angela?"

"No, we have not. We think this is the right thing to do," said Mr. Freeman. Looking directly at Mrs. Freeman, Sister said, "Are you sure?" Tawana Jo nodded in agreement with her husband. Labor Day being the next day, Sister told the Freemans she would arrange an appointment for the following day, Tuesday, September 2.

Sister telephoned Mrs. Thompson to arrange an appointment for the Freeman family. She informed Mrs. Thompson that Angela Freeman, age twelve, had given birth to a baby girl at home on Saturday, August 30, and that her parents requested the child be placed for adoption. Sister also said that the Freemans stated they were downtown shopping at the time of Angela's delivery, and that Angela had been babysitting her siblings.

On Tuesday, while Angela was still at St. Joseph Hospital, Broderick and Tawana Jo arrived on time for their appointment with Sister Teresa and Mrs. Thompson, the Director of Catholic Charities. Sister Teresa first gave the Freemans an overview of Catholic Charities of Shiawassee & Genesee Counties' services, assuming they knew little about the agency. Mr. Freeman's questions, directed to Sister, expressly focused on explaining the adoption process. The

Freemans were insistent that the child be placed for adoption immediately.

As Mrs. Thompson took notes for the adoption file, Sister told Mr. and Mrs. Freeman that she understood their request and that they accepted Catholic babies for care. "Since you are practicing Catholics, we can accommodate you. However," she warned, "Negro babies are extremely difficult to place. Often, they remain for years in boarding homes. In many cases," she said, "Catholic Charities is never able to place Negro babies."

"Many Negro families," she explained, "are fearful of adoption practices and for that reason fail to adopt even though they want a child. Here, we have a double problem," Sister said. "We would be looking for a Catholic family as well as a Negro family looking to adopt a child. Adoption for Negro babies is difficult," Mrs. Thompson emphasized again.

Sister asked, "Is it possible for the child to be placed with relatives? At least the baby would be in a permanent home much sooner than we could possibly locate one." Mr. Freeman said he understood, but that adoption was the only solution. Sister questioned whether there were any relatives who would be willing to accept the baby.

"Our relatives have no knowledge of Angela's pregnancy," her mother said, "And we intend to keep it that way. We do not want anyone to ever know about this."

Sister then questioned the Freemans about Angela's state of mind. "How does she feel about the child?" Sister asked.

"She refuses to discuss 'it,'" replied Mrs. Freeman.

"She told us she does not want 'it' at all," added Mr. Freeman.

"She only wants to return to school," Tawana Jo said.

"If there are no other arrangements," said Sister, "Catholic Charities is willing to accept the infant. However, we cannot promise that the child would be placed in an adoptive home. As a matter of fact, we have difficulty even finding boarding homes."

Mrs. Thompson then explained, "If you insist the child be placed for adoption, we have to define costs clearly."

"Okay, whatever it takes to get 'it' placed," Mr. Freeman said.

"If you insist the child be placed in a Catholic Charities boarding home, you will be required to pay twenty-five dollars for a layette, medical bills and other expenses. Catholic Charities will choose clothing and attend to the child's other needs. But, to be clear, the expenses will be charged to the two of you." Continuing, Mrs. Thompson said, "Room and board will amount to eleven dollars per week, which will also be your responsibility as well until the time of the court hearing."

Sister then asked if they were in a position to pay for these expenses. Broderick said, flatly, "We will have to." Sister explained that there will be a court hearing, what the hearing would include, the court date and who would have to be present. "Of course, Angela will need to be present and we would like the father to be there as well."

Angela's mother did not like the idea that her daughter would have to appear in court, but Sister went on to explain that, "As the child's mother, Angela has to be at the court hearing. There is no way around it. Angela must be at the hearing. After the hearing, the child will become Catholic Charities' responsibility."

"We understand," said Broderick, satisfied at accomplishing the desired outcome.

Mrs. Thompson's notes captured their appearance on that day, the third day after their daughter had given birth.

*Mr. Freeman is short in stature with a medium-brown complexion, brown eyes, and black hair. Mrs. Freeman is darker in complexion and also short in stature. She was very neatly attired in a maternity suit. Her hair was beautifully styled, and Mr. Freeman was also neatly dressed."*

*Mrs. Tawana Jo Freeman, age 32, was born in Chicago, Illinois. She completed high school and at one time was employed by Montgomery Ward.*

*Mr. Broderick Freeman, age 40, was born in Louisiana. He completed sixth grade in parochial school and after his military service went to work. He has remained employed at Chevrolet in Flint for the past 11½ years.*

Mr. and Mrs. Freeman currently have nine children, and Mrs. Freeman is presently seven months pregnant. Angela is the oldest. Violet, age 10, attends Stewart School and is in the sixth grade. Percella, age 8, attends Stewart School and is in the fourth grade. Pearlina, age 7, second grade. Broderick Jr., age 6, is in the first grade. Gail, age 5, is in the first grade. Evette, age 4, is in kindergarten and Randolph, age 3, is in pre-school. Sabella is 19 months.

## Seeking Solutions

*T*he next day, September 3, the Freemans met
with Catholic Charities caseworker Mrs. Constance
Edwards. Catholic Charities assigned Mrs. Edwards to
the Freemans because she herself was Catholic and a
Negro. Mrs. Edwards offered the Freemans a seat,
explained she had read Sister Teresa's and Mrs.
Thompson's notes and summarized them for the couple.
"I understand Angela, age twelve, has given birth to a
female child and that you are requesting the child be
placed for adoption. Is that right?"

Agreeing with the summary report, they both
acknowledged their desire to move forward with the
adoption. Mrs. Edwards opened her line of questioning
with "how could Angela have given birth to a full-term
baby if she did not gain any weight and did not show?"
Silence. "It would seem that with the many children you

have had, Mrs. Freeman, you could have readily determined Angela's condition." Again, silence. "You did not notice any morning sickness, nothing?" questioned Mrs. Edwards.

Blankly, Tawana Jo stated she had not suspected anything. "As a matter of fact," she blurted, "Angela had never caused us any trouble. She never leaves home unless taken by one of us. We just cannot figure out how anything like this could have happened."

Mrs. Edwards inquired as to the number of friends Angela had and with whom she associated in the neighborhood. Broderick said, "We don't allow her to have many friends." Uneasy, Tawana Jo broke in, saying, "She usually walks home from school with other youngsters in her class but she does not go out visiting. She likes being at home with us and she enjoys the smaller children. All the children are very close. Last year, on one occasion Angela attended a teen dance at school, but I drove her there and back."

Mrs. Edwards then asked, "How would you describe your daughter, Mrs. Freeman?"

"Shy, quiet, homebody," answered Tawana Jo. "She does not particularly care about going to the movies or anything of that sort unless the whole family attends." After a few moments of awkward silence, she said, "I do not understand how this could happen and I cannot possibly understand when it happened. My daughter is a good girl. She loves taking care of her younger siblings." Broderick sat silently, adjusting the cuff of his left shirt sleeve.

Mrs. Edwards asked, "Mr. Freeman, do you have anything to add? We need you both to help us. There are so many unanswered questions." Broderick shook his head slightly from side to side and said nothing.

Mrs. Edwards told them that she wanted to see Angela alone. Perhaps she would feel free to talk, she'd considered to herself. Perhaps she was fearful of talking with her parents in the room and would speak more freely without them. Tawana Jo asked why it was necessary for any adult to see Angela alone. She had thought that their discussion meant that everything would soon be concluded. As the parents of a minor, they would handle the situation from here. "Angela does not want to talk about it and only wants to forget," she said to Mrs. Edwards. "I think she should be left alone."

"Certainly, I could not work with Angela or try and help her without her knowledge, and for that reason I would have to see her."

"I do not want you to talk to her alone," said Broderick grimly. "You will not get any more information out of her."

"But Mr. Freeman . . ." protested Mrs. Edwards. Glaring, he interrupted her. "I disagreed with you seeing Angela alone. Sister had certainly tried, and we have, too," Broderick reasoned, "but Angela only wanted to talk about school, the types of clothing she wants, and how soon she can come home from the hospital."

Mrs. Edwards told the Freemans that perhaps what they were saying was true but that it was her responsibility to try. "If the baby were going to be placed for adoption we would certainly need information about the alleged father." Her comment was met with an uncomfortable silence. "I understood Angela has not mentioned who he is. Unless we can obtain some information, I am afraid we cannot accept the child. You have to understand that without this information the adoption could become more difficult. The adoptive parents would not know if or when the father might to want to reclaim custody of the child. Catholic Charities cannot place a child for adoption without all the necessary information." Speaking with finality, she said, "You do understand our hands are tied. We cannot move forward without having the father's consent as well as Angela's."

At that point Mr. Freeman looked over at his wife, took her hand in his and said, "I guess we will have to tell her."

"Tell me what?" Mrs. Edwards inquired.

"My oldest son, James, is the father," Broderick told her.

"James." Mrs. Edwards paused. "Please tell me about James." "James is twenty. He lives in New York City. He is about five foot six," brown complexion, and weighs about a hundred and forty pounds."

"What else can you tell me about him?"

"He attended a Catholic School until the ninth grade. He was working somewhere when I last heard from him. But it has been a while and I do not know what he is doing now." Clearing his throat, Broderick said, "James is my son from my first marriage."

Mrs. Edwards interrupted. "If James is in fact the child's father, do you realize he has raped your daughter? Angela is a minor." Tawana Jo sat grim-faced. "Oh, my God, you have to report him. You have to press charges against him. It is the law," Mrs. Edwards said, her voice rising in pitch. "He needs to pay for this." Mrs. Edwards paused to take a conscious breath and turned her attention to Tawana Jo. "Mrs. Freeman, what are you going to do about this? This is your daughter, your child, your baby." Before Tawana Jo could respond, Mrs. Edwards spun towards Broderick. "Mr. Freeman, what are you going to do about this? You have to do something."

Ignoring this, Broderick mentioned that "James lived with us when he was a very little boy, but he had not been in our home for quite some time until his visit during Christmas last year. But we have not seen or heard from him since."

"Undoubtedly, this must have been when, well, you know, took place" Tawana Jo said, staring down at the floor.

Firmly, Mrs. Edwards asked, "Mr. Freeman, what do you plan to do about this?"

"Well, I thought I would wait until he comes around and see what his story is."

"I do not understand why you are not pursuing charges against him. Why are you not upset? *Why?*" Her voice trailed off as she strove to regain her composure. "Are you going to at least require him to assume financial responsibility for the child, in that he is the adult and should be held accountable?" Broderick looked directly at Mrs. Edwards and said, placing deliberate weight on each word, "I'll wait until I see him."

Mrs. Edwards noticed that Angela's mother had a strange look on her face and had very little to say. "Mrs. Freeman, I don't understand why you are not willing to bring this man to justice for what he has done to your daughter." As Mrs. Edwards questioned her about what her husband had said about James and her daughter, Tawana Jo sat wordlessly, looking through Mrs. Edwards as though she were a phantom.

Finally, Tawana Jo said, "I don't know."

"I have to say I do not understand your decision, Mr. and Mrs. Freeman, and I must tell you I strongly disagree." Silence hung heavily in the room. "Please reconsider. Angela could suffer from this for the rest of her life."

"We have made our decision very clear and that's *that*," snarled Broderick. Taking his wife by the hand, he said, "It's time to go. Now!" As they stood to leave her office, Mrs. Edwards told the couple that after seeing Angela she would perhaps be getting in contact with them to obtain more information.

Both Broderick and Tawana Jo impressed Mrs. Edwards as being very much concerned about their daughter and very eager to have the whole matter settled and forgotten, but she later wrote *both acted very strange in regards to the alleged father*. Mrs. Edwards told her supervisor that, in her opinion, the Freemans were in fact "hiding something." They were evasive about how

Angela became pregnant, opposed to her speaking to Angela alone, adamant about not pursuing any legal action against James, the alleged father, and they did not appear to be angry. Their daughter was raped and they were not angry.

"That makes no sense to me," Mrs. Edwards said, her brow furrowing as she spoke to Mrs. Thompson. "Something about their story just does not add up, something is not right. Mr. Freeman's son has raped their daughter. She was pregnant and they say they did not know, but later, under pressure, they gave an explanation for the pregnancy. She has given birth to a child from that rape but they do not seem concerned about that—nor do they seem concerned about what lasting effects this might have on Angela. "It seems, in fact," Mrs. Edwards continued, absentmindedly flipping the pages of a notebook on her lap, "they are covering up something. I believe there is more to this than they are admitting."

"Yet they are certainly not accepting of what has happened," Mrs. Thompson observed. "Perhaps because both Angela and the father are in fact the Freemans' children, that would explain why this is impossible for Mr. and Mrs. Freeman to express their true feelings."

"Perhaps," said Mrs. Edwards. "But I am telling you, there's more to this. There's something."

That same evening Mrs. Edwards visited Angela at St. Joseph Hospital. She found a young child lying in bed, searching for explanations as to what had happened to her.

"Hello, Angela, my name is Constance Edwards. I am from Catholic Charities, and I am here to talk to you." Mrs. Edwards explained to Angela that she had spoken to her mother and father earlier that morning. She had come to see her, she said, because she was the person who would help her make plans for her baby. As she told her this, Angela began to cry. Placing her hand on Angela's, Mrs. Edwards said, "Don't cry, it's okay. Everything will be okay. I came by to see you and to ask you a few questions. I can also answer any questions you have."

Pulling her hand away, Angela sat in her hospital bed, silently looking towards the floor. Mrs. Edwards told Angela, "I understand that this situation must be difficult to talk about with your parents, because I am sure you must be afraid of being punished. But you can feel free to talk to me. I am here to help you." She remained silent. "Please, Angela, talk to me. I am your caseworker. I am here to help you. I know this is hard, but I can help. You have to talk to me." Angela said nothing.

Realizing that she could not reach Angela by talking about the baby, she asked if she was ready to go home from the hospital. Angela smiled and said, "I certainly am, and I am excited to start school." Proudly, she added, "School started yesterday, and I have never missed a day, not even a half-day." She began explaining that she told her mother the kind of skirts and matching tights she wanted and felt that she had enough sweaters. "So everything should be ready when I get home." She said she was very lonesome for her sisters and brothers and that she had never been separated from them. "Momma said they have been asking about me."

Mrs. Edwards commented to Angela that, being the oldest, she perhaps was a great help to her mother. Angela said she certainly was. "Because the children listen to me much better than they do Momma." Angela then laughed and said, "There are so many of them it is sometimes hard for Momma to keep up, but somehow I never have a problem with them. They know that Momma will punish them, but they misbehave anyway. They like me, and will do what I tell them."

Mrs. Edwards asked if she thought she might like to change schools to avoid the gossip that she may face if she returns to Whittier. Angela told Mrs. Edwards that her mother wanted her to go live with her aunt in Indiana and go to a school in her neighborhood. "Momma thinks it's a nice school. My aunt is a schoolteacher," Angela told her. "I want to be a schoolteacher, too, but I am not going unless the whole family goes." Mrs. Edwards commented that it would be difficult for the family to move because her father has a very good job here that supports the family. Mrs. Edwards told Angela that if she did go, her mother would arrange for her to come back and forth. "You would not lose touch with your family."

"If the whole family does not go," said Angela, stiffening, "I am not going."

Mrs. Edwards asked, "Which of your parents are you closer to? Your mother or your father?"

"I am close to them both. They both love me and I am a big help to them." She mentioned she has a lot of fun with her father building houses. Angela went on to explain that her father is a carpenter and not only had he built the home they live in, he had also built two others that he sold. "Whenever one of the houses is under construction, Momma and us kids help. The little ones cannot do much, but the older ones can. We work as a family."

Turning the discussion back to matters of current business, Mrs. Edwards explained that as soon as the baby is discharged from the hospital, she would be baptized. "Have you given any thought to a name? Angela, you are the baby's mother. You have the right to name her." Angela looked puzzled, as if she just then realized she was a mother. The smile drained from Angela's face and she again began to stare at the floor.

"Angela, would you like to name your baby?

After a long pause, Angela finally replied. "I don't think I would like that."

"Okay, would you like to keep the baby if your parents allowed you to?"

Angela shook her head to say no.

"Well, we need to get some information about the father of your child. I need your help, Angela, to make sure the baby has a healthy start. Can you please help me? Help your baby?" For the balance of the conversation, Angela remained quiet. She never once changed her facial expression and neither did she look up. When Mrs. Edwards was leaving, Angela told her that she appreciated her coming, and that she'd enjoyed the conversation.

"I am so sorry this happened to you. I wish you would let me help you. But I cannot help if you are not willing to talk to me." As tears began to trickle down her chubby cheeks, Mrs. Edwards turned and walked out of the room.

## Who's the Daddy?

*M*rs. Edwards described Angela to her supervisor as being of small stature, about five feet tall, dark brown complexion with thick black hair, which is of fairly good quality. "What struck me as most important," she said, "is her determination not to discuss her situation—perhaps it is a defense mechanism enabling her to forget what happened more easily. We have no knowledge as to whether Angela was forced into a sexual act or if she willingly participated. For that matter, we do not know when this started. We have no way of knowing why she refuses to talk. But we do know the law states that since she is a minor, Angela was raped. By who? That is the question."

Mrs. Edwards thought perhaps Angela could be traumatized, having suffered considerably during her pregnancy and in childbirth. "But surely she must have realized that something was happening to her body. Could she not feel the baby?"

"Perhaps she was being abused, or perhaps something was going on in the home no one knows about," speculated Mrs. Thompson. "Or perhaps she did not know during the early months that she was pregnant."

"Do you suppose she is mentally unstable?" asked Mrs. Edwards. "So many questions perhaps will never be answered," she murmured to herself, frustrated. Although she did not know for sure, Mrs. Edwards suspected foul play. "There is more to this than this family is willing to talk about," she grumbled. Mr. and Mrs. Freeman plan to say nothing more to Angela and seem to have no interest in pursuing legal action against James."

"In that regard," surmised Mrs. Thompson, "perhaps she will be able to forget the ordeal and continue her education as she desires. After all, she is only twelve. Perhaps this is the family's way of protecting her. We have to respect that."

"Maybe you are right," Mrs. Edwards said, "but I am telling you, something is wrong. I feel helpless."

"I agree, but we cannot do anything about that. What we *can* do is focus on making sure the baby is cared for and placed in a good home."

On the morning of Angela's last day in the hospital, Saturday, September 6, Sister Teresa came to visit her. Sister was determined to get Angela to reveal the father. Mrs. Edwards and the girl's own parents had been unsuccessful; however, Sister had a plan. After getting small talk out of the way, Sister asked, "Who is the father of your baby?" Angela refused to answer. However, with one last effort to get her to name the father, Sister said, "If you do not tell me who the father is, you will have to keep the baby. Angela said one word: "James." Sister demanded, "Are you *sure*?" Angela said nothing more.

Mrs. Edwards made an appointment to meet with Father Ryan, Priest of Christ the King Parish. Father had previously visited Angela, but she had refused to talk to him as well. Father Ryan stated that he was certainly shocked, as were her parents, as he had just seen Angela two weeks prior and that she did not appear to be pregnant. "It is almost impossible such a thing could happen without anyone knowing it," Father Ryan said to Mrs. Edwards. "Something seems off."

The priest stated that both Mr. and Mrs. Freeman had been married before and that Angela was not Mr. Freeman's child. Therefore, she was not related to the alleged father as had been assumed. "Mr. Freeman's first marriage was performed in the church and, naturally, having remarried, he cannot attend Sacraments. However, he had all the children baptized, and he attends Mass regularly. Mrs. Freeman," he continued, "is not Catholic; however, she attends Mass regularly. She has not objected to the children attending Mass and learning the Sacraments of Christianity.

Father had met James Freeman, the alleged father, and recalled that he had been in and out of the home but was usually getting into some kind of trouble. James had been living in New York for quite some time, so Father had not seen him recently. He recalled the Freemans mentioning that he did visit at Christmas last year.

Something else came to Father Ryan's mind. "Mr. Freeman was entirely different from his brother, who is also known to our parish. As a matter of fact, he is just the opposite. This Mr. Freeman, Angela's stepfather, takes care of his family and always sees to it that they have food, nice clothes and a loving home. He has never once asked the church for help. He is always willing to assist with different construction activities around the building and pitches in working with the other men of the church." At the time, Broderick was actually heading the group that was painting the church.

"He is a good man. Henry, Mr. Freeman's brother, is just the opposite, going from one agency to another for help and calling the church to get him out of jail. On several occasions, Henry would get angry and not show up at services for several months," Father explained.

"Angela is such a nice little girl," he said, changing the subject. "She has a bashful demeanor." Father said, "I am very sorry that this has happened, but I sincerely hoped Catholic Charities would be able to find a place for the baby." Mrs. Edwards told Father that Catholic Charities was having trouble finding a foster home and asked for his assistance in the search. "Of course, I will see what I can do. Let me make a few calls."

## Cover-Up

*M*rs. Edwards called Angela's mother to explain that she needed more information and asked if it would be possible to visit her at home. Tawana Jo said, "Absolutely, you are welcome to come." An appointment was scheduled for September 8. Before the scheduled appointment date, Tawana Jo called Mrs. Edwards to inquire whether she could assist her in helping to transfer Angela to another school.

"It seems the news had leaked out and had reached the school administrators as well as the students at Whittier," she told the social worker. "People are talking and we prefer Angela not return there. I also received a call from Mrs. Brown inquiring about the baby. The news appears to be traveling throughout the community."

Mrs. Edwards told Mrs. Freeman that she would discuss the situation with another member of Catholic Charities and see what could be done. Catholic Charities was able to get Angela transferred to Emerson Junior High School within that same week. The school, though located on the other side of town, would not be too difficult for Tawana Jo to drive Angela to.

On September 8, as planned, Mrs. Edwards arrived at the Freeman home and was greeted by Angela's parents and the younger children. The older ones were in school. Tawana Jo told Mrs. Edwards that she has had no problem getting Angela to school, and that she certainly appreciated Catholic Charities' assistance. The principal at Emerson did not think Angela would have any trouble, and there is only one girl in Emerson that knows Angela. "She seems to be adjusting to her new school," offered her mother. "She likes her classes and teacher. She even said the lunches are better," said Tawana Jo with a casual laugh.

The Freemans, noted Mrs. Edwards, were pleased with the transfer. But there was more to be discussed. She explained to the Freemans that Catholic Charities was very concerned about the background of the baby. "With James being Mr. Freeman's son, he would be a half-brother to Angela, and, as it is said, a child whose parents are closely related is often subject to some mental or physical illness." Mr. Freeman, could you provide us with more information about James's mother, and more information about yourself?"

It was at this point that Tawana Jo said "My husband is not Angela and Violet's father. I was married to Allen Blackmore in Louisville, Kentucky. Angela and Violet were born in that marriage. We divorced and the girls and I moved to Flint years ago." She was not positive about the exact date, and she seemed to have difficulty with most dates, Mrs. Edwards had observed, but she continued as best she could, saying, "Mr. Freeman and I were married in either 1950 or 1951 in Toledo, Ohio." With great confidence, she added, "All of the children, however, use the name Freeman, and that is how Angela is known. My husband's being Angela and Violet's stepfather has never made any difference with the children, and for that reason many people do not know that he is the stepfather of the older two," she said with a smile.

Mrs. Edwards said, "Thank you for the clarification. I would like to discuss Mr. Blackmore." Antagonistically, Tawana Jo said, "I do not see the relevance in discussing him."

"Mrs. Freeman, since he is Angela's father, it would help us to know his family history, education, and if there are any medical or psychological concerns we should be aware of, and . . ."

"No, there are not."

"Okay, well . . . can you tell me about his education? Do you know how we can contact him to get his medical history, education and family background?" Mrs. Edwards inquired.

"Absolutely not." And with that, Tawana Jo made it clear she was unwilling to discuss him any further. Changing the subject, she lightened her tone of voice, asking, "Can I get you something to drink? Would you like a cup of coffee? I have a pot on the stove."

"No, thank you, Mrs. Freeman." Turning her attention to Broderick, Mrs. Edwards inquired about his first marriage.

"I do not have anything to say about her," snapped Broderick, abruptly leaving the room." *What an odd, volatile man he is,* she thought to herself. Tawana Jo then told Mrs. Edwards that her husband was married in 1944 in Louisiana, and that his first wife's name was Virginia. One child, James, now age twenty, was born to them. They were later divorced. Taking notes, Mrs. Edwards soon had a brief biological sketch of James' mother. *Mrs. Virginia Freeman resides in Seattle, Washington. Mr. Freeman has lived in Flint for the past twelve years. His first wife is of light brown complexion, and she works somewhere in Seattle.*

"I have never met or spoken to her," volunteered Tawana Jo. "We do not hear from her directly and I do not know much about her."

As Broderick returned to the room, Mrs. Edwards tried to get more information regarding the first Mrs. Freeman's education, medical health and background. But Broderick was not interested in pursuing the subject and did not offer any information. Tawana Jo had stated all she knew. *Both Mr. and Mrs. Freeman appear to be people who prefer to remain silent about almost everything regarding their past marriages and Angela's child*, she noted.

"Mr. and Mrs. Freeman, I am sure this seems intrusive but these questions will help us to place Angela's child. We need family histories to complete the necessary paperwork. I would think if you want the child placed you would be more cooperative in helping us in this process." Both remained silent. *Angela closely identifies with her mother in this respect*, thought Mrs. Edwards.

When Mrs. Edwards stood to leave, she commented on the beautiful hardwood floors in the living room, and an attractive stone wall. Both Broderick and Tawana Jo eagerly spoke of having done the work themselves and talked about various other improvements they had made in the home. Tawana Jo said, "We have completed several interior remodels but we have yet to get to the basement." Broderick chimed in. "I plan to put a bedroom down there. I think that would be good for the children. Maybe Angela would like her own bedroom. What do you think, dear?" Broderick asked, turning to Tawana Jo with a smile. Mrs. Edwards, sensing that this might be an act put on for an audience of one—her—watched this exchange silently.

As Mrs. Edwards walked to her car, she thought about how the Freemans seem willing to talk as long as the conversation does not include their ex-spouses, James or the circumstances around Angela's situation. "Why?" As she drove toward her office she recalled their reactions to her questioning. It seemed baffling. Her gut told her something is wrong with this family. "What?"

Upon returning to her office, with perplexity, she penned the brief social history somewhat reluctantly disclosed to her by the Freemans. Her heart was unsettled by this family but she could do nothing except stay focused on placing the child. As a professional with a job to do, her attention turned to ensuring the delivery of the dependency petition to the court.

## Foster Care

*O*n Tuesday, September 9, I was removed from St. Joseph Hospital and taken to St. Michael's Church for baptism. I was given the name Catherine and baptized by Father Tom. Immediately following the ceremony I was placed in the foster home of Mrs. Wells.

On Friday, September 19, Angela's thirteenth birthday, Probate Court informed Mrs. Edwards that the hearing would be scheduled for Tuesday, November 18, at nine o'clock. Mrs. Edwards placed a telephone call to notify Angela's parents of the hearing date and gave them the judge's office location. On the call, Mrs. Edwards further explained that either she or Mr. Freeman could come along with Angela. Mrs. Edwards inquired whether either of them had spoken with James and if he would be attending the hearing.

"No, we have not," replied Tawana Jo.

Mrs. Edwards asked, "Do you intend to speak with him before the hearing? Since it is not until November, he would have time to arrange to attend."

"No, James will not be attending the hearing."

With parental rights pending, on Tuesday, September 30th, Sister visited me in Mrs. Wells' home. Mrs. Wells was a kind woman who had provided foster care for many children for Catholic Charities. As a favor to Father Ryan, she took me in, but at the time of his call she had six foster children. At one month old I had to be moved to a second foster home. Catholic Charities arranged for me to live with Mrs. Milton, who had also fostered several children and had provided a loving home for them. With two small children already in her care, she welcomed me into her home.

Mrs. Edwards arrived at court early on Tuesday, November 18, to await the Freemans. Shortly thereafter the Freeman family arrived, but Judge Doran was ill, and the hearing had to be rescheduled for Friday, November 21. Walking out of the courtroom, Mrs. Edwards informed the Freemans that I had been moved to a new foster home. She handed them an invoice for my expenses including a one-month infant medical checkup, housing, clothes and transportation. With Angela standing next to her, Tawana Jo took the bill and smiled. "Thank you," said Broderick. "We will take care of the bill." Taking his wife by the hand, they turned and walked away, with Angela following close behind.

Three days later, Mrs. Edwards, Mr. and Mrs. Freeman and Angela arrived in the court room at nine o'clock a.m. for the rescheduled hearing. Judge Doran talked at length with Angela about her home, school, her siblings, her parents and the baby. He described why they were in court stating, "We are here because you want to place your baby for adoption, right?" Looking at the wall, Angela shrugged her shoulders.

"Yes sir."

The Judge said, "My intent is to ensure you clearly understand exactly what is taking place today."

"Yes sir."

"Do you have any questions?"

"No sir, no questions."

"For the record, are you sure you want to place your baby for adoption, Angela?"

"Yes sir."

"Okay. Well, how is school?"

"Oh, I love school. I am doing very well."

"Has everyone at Catholic Charities helped you to understand the process?"

"Yes sir. I appreciate what Catholic Charities has done for us," Angela said happily.

While the Judge spoke with Angela, Mrs. Edwards approached Broderick. "We have additional accumulated expenses for the baby's care," she said to him. "We will send you the bill."

"I will take care of it," he replied.

Standing there with Angela's parents, Mrs. Edwards made a mental note that, as the grandparents, the Freemans showed no interest in the baby's welfare.

Months later, on Monday, February 16, 1959, Mrs. Edwards mentioned to Mrs. Thompson that she sees the Freeman family every Sunday at Mass. "The entire family appears very well dressed and they seem to be well adjusted and doing well financially. Angela seems to have put the ordeal behind her. I have not been able to speak with them after church but I will. I noticed in all these months the childcare costs have gone unpaid. Mr. Freeman assured me he would take care of the baby's medical bills and room and board expenses."

On a Sunday after church in April of 1959, Mrs. Edwards mentioned to Mr. Freeman that the invoices were still unpaid. "I will send the total payment shortly," he told her. Catholic Charities never received any money from the Freemans.

## Adoption

*O*ne day in early 1961, a couple showed up at the foster home where I was placed at the time. As they entered the front door, a voice called out to me as I ran to the top of the stairs to see who had come. At the top of the stairs looking down at them, I immediately recognized the neatly dressed couple had come to visit me before. I remember because I was very sad the last time I saw them because my dolls head had come off and I could not fix her. "Come down, Catherine, and see who is here to see you," I heard someone say. I came down the stairs, looking at the couple.

Happily pointing at the jump rope the man was holding, I said, "You're the man that fixed my doll!" His big smile was soft and soothing. I immediately recognized the man as the person who fixed Trudy, my prized possession. I was drawn to him, thinking of him as the man who took care of my best friend.

As I slowly walked down the stairs, he stretched his arm out and presented the jump rope to me. I hugged him with a heart of gratitude. That man, Lamont Wyatt, became my adoptive father. His wife, Malinda Wyatt, became my adoptive mother.

Time passed, I adjusted to my family as best I could. When I was about eight, my adoptive grandmother, who was living with us at the time, was angry with me one day for doing something childish. Suddenly she screamed the word "adoption" at me. Her words were something like "and you were adopted." She tended to rattle on and I never paid too much attention to her long-windedness unless she said something worth listening to. But when she said that word, my heart stopped.

*Adopted, what is that?* I remember thinking. My grandmother was wonderful to me, though when she lived with us I had to share my room with her. As a child I came to expect my grandmother to provide that much-needed spare change so I could buy candy or a popsicle from the ice cream truck. She'd prepare wonderful, home-cooked Grandma-kind-of meals, especially her skillet-fried potatoes and, OMG, those syrup, butter, and bread lunches. I gain five pounds just thinking about them. I also recall how she made me do chores around the house. The lessons I learned from my grandmother are endless, and some—persevere, work hard, trust God—helped me get to where I am today.

Perhaps the most important lesson I learned from her was through observing her strength and independence. My Beech-Nut Tobacco-chewing grandmother was a very large part of my life. She was the one who was there each day when I came from school. She saw the torment I received daily and taught me how to fight the neighborhood bully, who intimidated, taunted and chased me home every day on the way home from school. She told me to put some heavy rocks in my purse and advised me how to handle the situation.

"The next time that girl chases you home," she said, "you stand your ground. Do not run and do not say a word. Let her think you are scared, but when she swings at you, you hit her as hard as you can with your purse." Needless to say, I never had any more trouble out of that bully. Thanks, Gran!

Although she was not my father's favorite person, there was a comforting consistency in her ways. It was not uncommon for her to show anger, though when she did, I probably had done something worthy of it. But on this particular day, I wasn't going to ask her what "adopted" meant. I waited impatiently until my mother came home.

As Malinda walked across the threshold of the house, I unleashed a torrent of questions. "Am I adopted? What is 'adopted'? Am I sick? Momma, what is 'adopted'? What's wrong with me?" My questions took her by surprise and she tried to discourage them, but I was stubbornly persistent, demanding her attention as I followed her through the house seeking answers.

"Who told you?" she demanded.

"Gran."

I cannot remember the exact reason for my grandmother's anger and what led to the words she'd said so harshly, but I do remember being a very young, confused and vulnerable child. My mother and grandmother had argued many times during my childhood because my grandmother did not like the fact that I was left-handed and she insisted my mother make me use my right hand. Thankfully, my mother did not agree.

Of course, my mother was angry at my grandmother for telling me, because I am sure that was not the way my parents had wanted me to find out. But it was out. After scolding my grandmother, Malinda reluctantly said, "Yes, you are adopted." I recall that it seemed to pain her to have to tell me.

As young as I was, I remember looking through her hijacked essence as an unspoken something passed between us—an indistinguishable disturbance from which she and I would never recover. It changed me, and I believe she felt it. Whatever it was, it was not a good thing, and it perhaps signaled the beginning of the distance that would continue to dwell between us.

Throughout my childhood, I always felt as though my adoptive mother cared more for my brother, Sherman, than she did for me, but I could not understand why. What was it about me? What was it about *him*? The explanation of adoption rested solely on her. It was on her to explain it to me, and it was on her to explain it to me until I understood. She tried to explain adoption but her words just made me feel more different and farther away from her. I needed connection and a sense of togetherness, but that experience was not the case.

The next day, her admission that I had been adopted was still very troubling to me. It was not something that I could let go. I would not let it go. Clearly, the subject was not something she cared to discuss. But I was relentless in my questioning. And so, over the course of the next few days, I continued to have many questions.

"Does adopted mean I have a disease?" What is a foster home? How long was I in foster homes? Is that where you got me from?

"Does adopted mean you paid for me? Was I the only girl you visited in foster homes? How old was I when you adopted me?

"Why did you adopt me? Why was I given away? Is something wrong with me?

"Does adopted mean I am not your daughter? Does adopted mean I am not daddy's daughter, either? Does adopted mean you are going to give me back?

"Where is my *real* family? Where is my *real* mother? Do you know my real family?"

Then I asked, point blank, "Is Sherman adopted?" But before those words landed on her heart, the deeper question sprang from my lips: "Is that why you love him more?" With that, my questions stopped.

An uncomfortable silence emerged, hanging in the air like smog. Searching for a reason, in my young mind, I believed my brother was her biological son. That would explain her affection towards him. At least, that's what I thought. Although the word "adopted" was incomprehensible to me and I had so many more questions, it was my question about Sherman that ultimately messed me up.

"Yes, he is adopted," my adoptive mother said quietly.

I cried.

Her words broke me. My desecrated essence shifted inside me. Once I learned the truth, there was nowhere I could hang my hurt. Her words introduced me to immeasurable pain, pain that still exists today. But it is not the result of having been abused or neglected, because I was not. I had everything other kids had. I just did not have her. I craved a mother's love. I needed my mother to mother me because I needed that role model. I needed a mother's love to show me the foundation of what true unconditional love is.

I wanted girl time, special time with her, so I could feel important, too. I did not have that, but I needed it so desperately. That was the one important thing she could have given me; instead, it was denied me. She gave her love and time to my brother. This was not because of any biological connection that made her feel closer to Sherman; it was because she just cared for him more, and she showed it.

My mother and grandmother were very close as well. I knew that family history was an important issue between them. They would scratch each other's scalp while spending hours recalling their family ancestry. Looking through old photo albums, recounting times of yesteryears past, seemed to bring them so much joy. I wanted that mother-daughter bond I witnessed between them. Not having that foundational connection made it difficult to entrust my heart to others.

In my young mind I surrendered to the fact that her heart had room for one child, and I was not that child. In order to handle the pain of my reality, I had to hang the hurt somewhere. The only place to hang it was on me. I was left to deal with unexplainable pain at the vulnerable age of eight. On my own, with Trudy, my plastic, secret-keeping forever friend, I felt adopted as I watched my mother mothering my brother. Consequently, throughout my childhood and throughout my difficult teens, I bore the pain.

Not long after adopting me at age three, my parents put me in tap, ballet, modern and jazz dance classes. Dance later became one of the most important gifts they ever gave me. It became my outlet, my refuge, my safe space my way to cope. The structure and creativity of dance filled a void deep within me. I became passionate about dance. As an art form I could actively pursue, it increased my self-esteem, providing an outlet for self-expression.

I was good at it, but it was hard work, requiring a discipline that shaped my life's view. Through the challenges of learning dance, the twice-weekly participation in the rote techniques of the art form, I gained confidence that I transferred to the emptiness I felt. In the music, and through movement and expression, I felt love.

My father, Lamont, was an enjoyable man to be around when I was young. My young friends called him the "black Kentucky Fried Chicken man" because he looked just like the Colonel. My father had many friends and they came over to our house often. All of my father's friends were nice. They always seemed to have a drink of some kind. They enjoyed laughing and smoking fat cigars. My father drank all kinds of beer, but bourbon, vodka and Crown Royal whiskey were his favorites. He drank often. He drank a lot.

When I was a young girl, my father was my big, brave hero who could do anything, and he always made me feel special. My father made driving through the car wash an exciting experience. I loved going through the car wash. It was always over too quickly. I think it also had to do with the fact that I was with him, and believed him to be the best man on earth. He would take me to the nearby Coney Island drive-in restaurant, where I got to press the button and wait for the voice on the other end of the box to speak. Boy, I thought that was awesome and that my daddy was a genius. When the food arrived, he always ordered a big chocolate milkshake just for me. I would sit with milkshake in hand, straw in mouth, and love in my heart for my daddy. He would drive down the street with the music of

B.B. King, Little Walter, Howlin' Wolf or Muddy Waters blasting. The blues was his thing. He'd whistle and snap his fingers to the tunes of Ray Charles, Otis Redding and Sam Cooke, and I would smile. He seemed happy most of the time, which made me happy. With the absence of my mother's love in my life, my father's doting attention and time was magical to me.

As I grew older, our relationship began to change. The once-happy- natured Daddy I knew became different. He still listened to the blues but it became the darker side of the blues—more about drinkin', cheatin', and leavin' and less about livin' and lovin'. I began to realize his drinking was a problem in our home. He seemed happiest among his friends, away from his wife and family. My dad became less protective, less of a parent altogether.

That vulnerable child in me wanted to be close to my father. I needed connection, family foundation, stability, security . . . lasting love. I needed protection—from what exactly, I do not know—but feeling so alone in my home, I needed my father. He was there physically but he was not there emotionally. Physically, he handed out punishments, sometimes money, but he was emotionally void, ill-equipped. Suggestions, fatherly advice, recommendations based on his experience were not something he was willing or able to give. It was only after I was well along in high school, learning about World War II, did I discover that he fought alongside General George Patton.

While studying World War II, I happened to mention that the next day I would be tested on this subject. My mother said, "Go in the bedroom and ask your dad about Patton. He knew him in the army." My father was a mystery, but he was the reason my family became Catholic. He told my mother that during the war, on the battlefields filled with blood and death, he could see priests giving last rites, praying with and over the soldiers, dying on the battlefield unarmed and serving God. He told her their faithful acts of compassion and sacrifice impressed him so much that he insisted on becoming Catholic.

My parents were raised in the Baptist church, but Malinda agreed that if he would go to church she would become Catholic. When they adopted me, they—along with Sherman—had already completed the church's required classes. Adoption was never a topic of discussion with my father.

Sherman and I grew up having the kind of relationship common to most siblings of differing genders. Being the oldest, he kicked my butt in earlier years and protected it in later years. He and I went to Catholic school during our early elementary years. We were two black kids attending Saint Francis of Assisi, an all-white Catholic school, so he had to fight a lot—sometimes on my behalf, most times on his own behalf. We encountered many racial problems at Saint Francis. The nuns were of no help. To be honest, on most occasions they did nothing when they could have prevented our mistreatment by the white children.

My recollections of those days are more about survival rather than getting an education. As a matter of fact, I do not recall learning much at all. I struggled with multiplication, always lost at the spelling bee, and was laughed at constantly. The kids were mean. I mean they were *really* mean. At six and seven years old I had no friends at school, not one. No one talked to me. No one ate lunch with me. No one played with me on the playground. I did not understand why no one liked me. At that age, I did not know or understand discrimination or racism, but nevertheless I felt its wrath every day.

Standing in line preparing to march into Mass each morning was when I felt most comfortable. We were just a line of kids on our way to church. No talking, no pushing, no cutting line, no getting out of line, hands to yourself. No one could hurt me in that line. Under the cover of Catholic school and drilled daily with Catholic doctrine, behavior and beliefs, one priest stands out in my mind as someone who tried to make things comfortable for me: Father Mike. I remember the day before I was to go into the hospital to have my tonsils removed; Father Mike pulled me out of line, placed his hands on each side of my throat and prayed over me. Then he told me to go get back in line. Off to Mass I went.

## Her Truth, My Truth

$A$doption set the tone for my mental wellbeing as a child. By the age of six, I knew I was definitely not my mother's child of choice. There is a huge difference between "like" and "love", and there were many times throughout my childhood when it was crystal clear that she liked me, but she loved him. Feelings of separateness, different, not quite equal, "less than" were infused in my psyche and had become my constant companion.

My adolescence and teenage years were stained with the favoritism my mother bestowed on my brother. Misbehaving to get her attention, unfortunately, proved to widen the gap. Envious of the strong relationship and deep affection, I witnessed between them, often left me wondering was it my big lips, nappy hair, pug nose, dark skin, or chubby thighs? When I complained or asked

"Why do you love him more" her rational was "He needs me more." That was her truth.

Family vacations, gatherings, parties, and picnics were always overshadowed by my inner pain. By 1976, my senior year in school, I was filled with immense emptiness. Everywhere I turned, I felt as though I didn't belong. At eighteen, I eagerly left home to attend college in Hartford, Connecticut. Leaving home, I reasoned, removed me from a place I never felt wanted and would allow me to find who Catherine was, where Catherine belonged, and what Catherine wanted.

Learning my way around and making new friends came easy; however, the emptiness I thought I left behind, followed me. College life became much more than hanging-out with the friends I'd made, dance classes, piano lessons, Kinesiology, practice and rehearsals. In the quiet of my dorm room, alone, I began to examine the emotional minefields in my life.

Like peeling an onion, I began to expose layer upon layer of previously concealed facts that at times, I admit, left me seething. There in my room, I recalled one such layer which revealed the deceitful inconsistencies I grew up believing regarding the circumstances of my birth and subsequent adoption. For decades, those conflicting and dubious details had lingered in the air like a musty fog.

Months after discovering adoption was a part of who I am, my heart remained unsettled. In yet another round of inquiries, I asked my mother another life-altering question. I wanted to know, I had to know, I was determined to find out if she knew anything about the woman who had given birth to me. At first she hesitated, refusing to talk about it. "You need to drop it," she'd say. "It doesn't matter," she'd say. But of course, it mattered to me. Relentlessly, I refused to give up on questioning her. I believed I had a right to know.

Worn down by my insistent questioning, she told me that a nun had given her a small piece of information about my biological mother. She said the nun told her that my birth mother was a young, single woman from New York, a high-profile secretary who had fallen in love with a married man. After a brief affair that eventually resulted in pregnancy, the man broke off the affair. She wanted to keep the child, while he demanded she get rid of it — *me*. Married with children of his own, he wanted nothing more to do with her or it.

She found herself single, pregnant, Catholic and alone. An abortion, although uncommon at the time, was not something her faith would allow her to consider. This nameless woman could not bear to embarrass her family, so she came to Flint late in her pregnancy to give birth to me at a Catholic hospital — St. Joseph. My questions to my adoptive mother as to why the nameless woman came to Flint went unanswered.

Melinda claimed that the nun had also told her it was the Catholic agency's custom to contact the biological mother six months after the delivery (providing they were given accurate contact information) to see if the mother had changed her mind and wished to be reunited with her child. As it was told to me, this nun had placed a call to my biological mother six months after my birth, inquiring into her health and financial status and to see if she did, in fact, want to be reunited with her child.

My adoptive mother, looking straight into my eyes, went on to utter words that cut to the core of me. According to her, my mother's words to the inquiring nun were as follows: "I told you, I don't want that damn baby. I don't want anything to do with it. Don't call me again." My biological mother hung up the phone, I was told, and that was that. The nuns then placed me in the foster care system of Catholic Social Services. At the impressionable age of eight, my very being was inflamed by her words, which landed on my heart with the thud of falling boulders. Pain echoed through my soul. That was her truth.

As I recalled her pain filled words laying on my dorm room bed, tears streaming down each side of face, on that cold wintery Connecticut day, I said out loud, to myself, "Why do you feel as though you are unequal, "less than", not good enough? Why the hell are you wearing someone else's crap?" As I boiled with anger, I asked myself, "Catherine, are you going to continue to allow her to emotionally destroy you or are you going to accept yourself for who you are and realize you are all you got?"

The aloneness of my dorm room gave me time to learn about *me* and become secure in my inner strength. In the stillness, in listening past the darkness, I discovered what was best for me and how I was going to live. Looking at my life, often through painful tears, I came to terms with my mother's truth, eliminated it, and embraced *my truth*.

Life happened as the years flew by and my last semester approached. It was with trepidation that I returned home. But I was different. Changed. Among lessons learned, I had found self-acceptance, independence and inner strength. I had changed my perspective, realizing I didn't need external approval or acceptance.

My independence and home life were at odds from the first moment I returned home, proving to be extremely uncomfortable. Determined to get out of that house, I quickly moved to Richmond California, and got a job teaching dance in Oakland at the community center. Teaching dance to the kids allowed me to pour into their lives something I didn't have. But, unable to afford California living, a year later I made the hard decision to return home.

It was the early 1980's. The "Great Recession" crippled Flint. Jobs were scarce. Nonetheless, I managed to land a job at the YMCA, got married, and move out. I used this marriage as a distraction and embraced motherhood. Eighteen months later Jonathan was born. Three months later my father died and Aaron was born the following year. Three years later Jalyon was born. I bought a house, got a job working for General Motors, divorced my deadbeat husband and got a dog.

Shortly thereafter, I met Tim at work. We were married fifteen months later. Finally, my house became a home. My children's smiles filled my heart, as my soul mate and I built a loving and, what I thought would be, a trusting lasting "happily ever after". Both laid off from General Motors we moved our family to Tennessee in 1990 to work at Saturn General Motors. The following few years were happy, but in 1994, the soundtrack of our harmonious lives were altered, *forever* destroyed by secrets, silence, lies, and betrayal.

That year gave new meaning to the word "catastrophic"—which, for the next five years, defined our home. For my three children, it was also the beginning of a period in which their lives would be reshaped, transformed in more ways than a mother's heart could surely bear. It began on April 12$^{th}$, the day my family was shattered.

While seated in the crowded waiting room of my OB-GYN, my husband, Tim, tried to console me. I was in so much pain from a hysterectomy I had undergone two weeks prior, my skin felt as if it were on fire. Finally, Tim went to tell the receptionist that we were leaving. She informed the doctor and we were hurriedly escorted to his office. Anxiety gripped Tim visibly, as we sat quietly waiting for the doctor to enter the room.

Recovery from the excruciating surgery had left me weak, miserable, oozing blood through the bandages, and in pain. Glancing up to see my doctor entering the room, I immediately saw the grim expression on his face. My doctor, having known Tim and me for years, told us that I had tested positive for the "human immunodeficiency virus"—HIV, the virus that causes acquired immunodeficiency syndrome (AIDS).

Dread consumed me. His sledgehammer diagnosis exploded over me, as fear suddenly took my imagination to all the grisly images of AIDS and the dark unknown that now lay before me. Bewildered, I asked him, "Why was I tested? Who tested me?" He avoided my questions, focusing only on my well-being. I began to feel nauseated. The room began to spin, as I told him he had to be mistaken. A long moment passed as my life flashed before me. It was only supposed to be a simple hysterectomy, not HIV! *Not AIDS!* I gasped for air, holding my pain-soaked stomach. I felt as if I had been delivered into the hands of hell. In the midst of thinking of my faithfulness to my husband, instantaneously my thoughts turned to my children. The thought of leaving them motherless overwhelmed me. Finally, resigned to the fact, I said, "What do we do now?"

Silent eye contact between Tim and I was broken as he turned to the doctor and said that he should be tested. The doctor agreed and immediately contacted the adjoining hospital. We left his office in silence and walked slowly to the car, where I sat astounded, wondering what had just happened. As Tim walked over to the hospital to have his blood drawn, I struggled to recall the doctor's words, realizing my life had changed forever. Sitting alone in the passenger's seat of the car, replaying recent events, my thoughts ran to my children.

While I anxiously waited for his results, praying he would be HIV negative, I educated myself. I read articles, stories, medical journals, papers, brochures, books, magazines, flyers, anything I could find, most of which pertained to HIV/AIDS in men. Quickly grasping HIV terms, I found myself using words such as opportunistic infections, symptomatic, asymptomatic, viral loads, T-cell counts, and T-8 ratios.

On the day he was scheduled to get his results, Tim refused to go to his doctor's appointment. Instead, I went in his place, and, sadly, I was told my husband was HIV-Positive. Robotically, I drove home. Slowly, painfully climbing the stairs to our bedroom, I found Tim, his back to me, lying in bed. As I delivered the heart-wrenching news that his tests were positive, he turned, our eyes locked, and I looked into his hijacked soul, as an unspoken something passed between us. Telling him this news collapsed my world.

A few days later, at his first infectious disease appointment, Tim was placed on Azidothymidine (AZT), the only medication known in 1994 to treat HIV/AIDS. He became consumed by defeat, anger, and frustration. I saw him surrender to the bottom of a vodka bottle, escaping our devastating reality as our marriage crumbled under the weight of deceit.

As time passed, I became broken, bone-crushingly depressed. I felt hopeless, scared, and alone. I was engulfed by the heaviness, the burden of HIV. Lost in the diagnosis, I could think of nothing else. Reaching for support, I met with my employer's medical director, the priest at my church, and, finally, my mother. In each case, I was met with rejection. I did not realize I would eventually lose everything: my job, my health insurance, my car, my church family, my home, my friends, my weight, my confidence, my marriage, my sleep, my appetite, my self-esteem, what little support my mother could muster, and, according to my prognosis, I could expect to lose my life.

As the foundation of our family crumbled, slaughtering my soul, incinerating my home, and cannibalizing my marriage, my children were all that mattered to me. I wanted desperately to protect them from the road ahead. I coped by writing letters to them. Struggling with the specter of dying from a disease that carried entrenched stigma, through countless spiral-bound notebooks, I detailed my love for each of them and why the thought of leaving them was destroying me more than the disease. Unveiling my deepest heartbreak to them paled in comparison to what I imagined they would endure upon their parents' deaths.

My marriage was in ruins, and my children were always in the forefront of my every thought. My letters to them intensified. Isolated and alone, yet trying to keep a brave front, I was always mindful of their trauma and the sorrow HIV/AIDS was yet to bring them. The letters to my children, since the first day of my diagnosis, kept me sane in the insanity of HIV.

It was during that time early in my diagnosis that I gave birth to a nonprofit organization named "Women On Maintaining Education and Nutrition" (W.O.M.E.N.). I established W.O.M.E.N. because there were no HIV/AIDS services formulated specifically for heterosexual HIV-Positive women of color like me in my community.  W.O.M.E.N.'s first program began as a small support group named "Women On Reasons To Heal", (W.O.R.T.H.) in a bedroom of our Brentwood home. With a growing membership, women from as far away as Paducah, Kentucky and Birmingham, Alabama came with the objective of offering HIV-Positive women, mothers, and their families encouragement through difficult times, while celebrating each of life's joys.

With my children's encouragement, and to the disgrace of my mother, I began speaking publically. I produced a video, *Reasons To Live; Women Their Families and HIV,* which premiered at Vanderbilt Scarritt Bennett Center in 1996 to a packed audience. I filed for divorce that same year. Trying to keep my children grounded amidst the overwhelming changes became more and more difficult, because the stigma of AIDS had already dehumanized me, taken from me, encapsulated me, and engulfed my soul. I had no one to turn to for help. I was extremely sensitive to the children's bewilderment, uncertainty, and pain, which became more important than anything HIV could ever do to me. I had to be strong for them.

As my public appearances expanded, *AIDS Memoir Journal of an HIV Positive Mother,* taken from the letters written to them, was published, in 1997. Important to me was keeping my children close, ensuring they traveled with me to most speaking events. In succession, my second book, *Positive People*

*Combating HIV/AIDS,* and third book *My Life With AIDS Tragedy to Triumph* were published.

Emboldened, empowered or perhaps stupid, I pushed back against what I saw as a well-oiled, good-ole-boy political network narrative which swallowed local HIV/AIDS funding resulting in resource shortages among communities of color.

So, where there was no voice for women of color living with HIV/AIDS in my community, I became that voice. Where there was no women-centered HIV/AIDS programming, I created it. Where there was no women-centered support group, I formed one. Where there was no food pantry to meet the needs of HIV-Positive women of color, I organized one. Where there was no massage therapy, holistic care, and nutrition services, I produced them.

Where there was no youth-centered education service for the children of HIV-Positive women of color, I created one. Where there was no outreach targeting communities of color, I designed it. Where there were no culturally competent HIV testing, counseling and supportive services for HIV-Positive women of color and their partners available in the heart of Nashville, I implemented them. Where there were no other women of color living with HIV/AIDS in my community who were mentors, and role models for other HIV-Positive women, I became one. Where there were no services which linked HIV-Positive women of color in the United States to HIV-Positive African women living in Nigeria, I linked them. I saw the needs and I made it happen.

As a student of my mother's truth, my husband's betrayal, hell, life itself, I learned the hard lessons of what it takes to really, truly be unmoved, and determined. That is *my truth*!

## The Search

*F*inding my biological mother became essential. . but I had no idea what to do. I did not know what the first steps were, who to call, or whether my adoption was "open" or "closed"; that is, whether my file was accessible or whether it was sealed.

The search for my biological mother began in front of my computer on January 1, 1998, after spending the previous holiday in deep reflection regarding those areas of my life which I had neglected. In that much-needed quiet time, I remembered the barrage of childhood questions I'd hurled at my adoptive mother and hearing her tell me that my adoption had been handled through Catholic Charities in Flint. So, I started there.

I learned that all Michigan adoptions have a corresponding court record and are required to also have an agency record. Michigan's adoption law requires that adoption agencies, the Department of Human Services, and the probate courts all maintain and release information, when requested, from adoption records in their possession. In most cases, information from closed adoptions can be released to the adult adoptee, the adoptive parents of a minor, and a biological parent or adult biological sibling. The type and amount of information released could vary. But under the law I was at least entitled to receive "Non-Identifying Information." Depending upon the circumstances, I could perhaps receive "Identifying Information." In the process, I would have to file a petition to gain access to my records.

A chain of phone calls led me through a network in which one person led me to another who, in turn, would lead me to someone else. So the following week I sent a written inquiry to Catholic Charities and got back to the business of my life. Three weeks later, in late January, a kindhearted woman within Catholic Charities Of Shiawassee and Genesee Counties called me to inform me she had received my request and my case would be assigned to an individual from Confidential Intermediary Services, a external independent agency that assists adult adoptees with the process of locating biological parents.

During the conversation I was also made aware of the $250 administrative, filing, handling and copying fees. A few weeks after the payment had been processed, I received a call from another Catholic Charities case manager, who informed me that I would receive forms by mail which I needed to complete. The packet would also explain the process and my rights under Michigan law. I would need to complete them, get them notarized, and FedEx them back to her.

After I completed the first set of documents, I received a second set. Returning them, I received a third. Another batch of documents soon arrived . . . and then another. As the back-and-forth, back-and-forth, back-and-forth process continued, I waited, and waited, and waited some more, becoming extremely disappointed, frustrated and emotionally drained.

Then in May of that year, I was contacted by a Confidential Intermediary Services worker who took my case to heart after I poured my heart out to her regarding the process, telling her about my HIV diagnosis and the urgent need I had for finding closure. After waiving a three hundred dollar Confidential Intermediary Services fee, the enthusiastic service worker filed my request in the court and began the long-awaited search.

Several months passed, and her efforts during that time proved to be fruitless. I had provided names, telephone numbers and addresses of anyone and everyone I believed could possibly provide information to aid her in her search efforts. Dead end after dead end fueled her own frustration with a maze of disconnected telephone numbers and unanswered letters that led her smack-dab into a brick wall: the barrier of a closed-mouthed older generation of folks who were unwilling to discuss family secrets from the past. The early-twentieth-century culture in which they had been raised had trained them to be uncomfortable discussing such private matters.

Keeping me informed, she diligently persisted. In March of 1999 she sent me a response which stated the Genesee County Probate Court had received and was reviewing my request for the release of my adoption file. Then, an ongoing assortment of various delays—lost files, misplaced documents, re-filings, and personnel changes times three, in addition to the ongoing chaotic busyness of my own life as a working mother, author, and activist, slowed the process to a crawl.

Finally, three years later, in June 2000, a new Confidential Intermediary Services worker who had been assigned my case and had pursued it with tenacity telephoned to say she had pushed through existing barriers and had mailed me a document labeled "Non-Identifying Information." Three days later in late June, my hands shook as my tear-filled eyes quickly moved across lines of text which described nameless people. Although I was grateful, it was at best a vague sketch of my family of origin, leaving out vital details. While the document did not give me the identifying information I would need in order to locate actual people, it did provide me the fortitude to proceed.

From the two-and-a-half-page document I was able to determine that my unnamed mother was born in Kentucky and moved to Flint when she was young; she was the oldest of eight siblings. My grandparents were unaware of their daughter's pregnancy and were downtown shopping when I was born. My maternal grandmother was divorced from my maternal grandfather and no medical information was made available about him.

Further, my maternal grandmother's current husband was born in Louisiana and had a twenty-year-old son born from a previous union. The information-deprived file hurt me deeply, as its blank spaces only amplified long-unanswered questions. *What is my mother's name? Is she alive? Who is she? Where is she? How can I find her?* Emptiness embraced my heart.

Six exhausting years since I had set off on this journey, with the assistance of the fifth consecutive Confidential Intermediary Services worker, I successfully petitioned the court to unseal my records, and I was finally granted the right to have my adoption records unsealed. The next document I received was the "Identifying Information." My heart beat with fury as I pulled the package out of the mailbox and read the return address label. "Oh my God," I gasped. "It's finally here."

Stone-faced and determined not to cry, I walked slowly towards my front door. My trembling hands found the edge of the envelope as I tore it open to reveal my family history—magnificent yet devastatingly brutal typed pages exposing details of my past that had long been withheld from me stopped me in my tracks. My eyes slowly embraced the pages, my brain processing each word. Giving in to the deep meaning of the words on those pages, oh, how my soul began to wail.

Standing in my driveway, I held my stomach as my cries engulfed me, rising from some unknown place inside me. Eyes glazed, hands wrenched, snot running, groaning, sobbing, I desperately tried to catch my breath as I interpreted the information: my mother, my father, uncles, aunts, grandparents, and the circumstances behind my being placed for adoption.

In anguish, my spirit grieved. I walked the floor, head pounding, heart racing, hands shaking, I collapsed on the living room floor as I tried to absorb the story of my life unfolding in my hands.

Howls sang out from a low place within me as my mind-will-emotions—the totality of my very essence— mourned each piece of news. The process I had so earnestly sought had now, finally, become vividly real. In a puddle of tears I sat on the floor, absorbing my family background: names—especially the name of my biological mother—schools, grandparents' names, siblings' names, ages and even their home addresses all stood at attention.

I cried, I read, I cried and read some more as the story of my life's beginning became real. My mother, age fourteen. *What! Age fourteen!* I stopped reading. "My God, she was a baby," I said, as long, wailing cries emanated into the air, as air itself became difficult to catch.

As my chest heaved and tears blinded my eyes, my body gradually became weak. Finally I had her name, her description, her background, her parents, her life . . . and then a realization flashed across my mind—

she didn't know *my* name. It suddenly occurred to me that I knew more about her than she did me—or at least I believed that to be the case. As I stared down at the tear-stained pages that told my story, I wept woefully because my own mother did not know my name. Throughout the adoption file, the words "it" and "the baby" pierced my core as I realized those words were describing a nameless me.

Between breaths I thought of the many times over my life that nurses, doctors, and hospitals, asked me about my family medical history. *Do you have a history of cancer, asthma, stroke, diabetes?* My response had always been, "I'm adopted." I always placed a big N/A and skipped that section on the form.

Then my thoughts turned to my birth certificate. Not the document I had been given and had used all of my life, but the *real* birth certificate. With all the identifying information I'd received, I did not get an official birth certificate. Pulling myself together, I placed a call to the Confidential Intermediary Program worker and asked for a birth certificate with a certified seal. I was informed that none existed. She told me I had received all the information the court had on record and I should continue to use the birth certificate I had been given that listed my adopted parents.

## I Am Your Mother

*I*t took a year for me to come to terms with the
information in my adoption file, which I read parts of to
Trudy regularly. In the middle of a hectic morning in the
spring of 2004, I received an email; the subject line
stated, *I'm looking for D. Wyatt. Can you help me?*
Usually, I would have deleted such an email, but because
it had my name "Wyatt" in the subject line, I opened it. I
replied, "I can't help find D. Wyatt, but I am C. Wyatt
and I'm looking for my biological mother." For the life of
me, I cannot explain why I wrote those words to
someone I did not know. With no idea as to who was on
the other side of the email, I pushed "send" and forgot all
about it. The morning moved quickly with meetings,
calls, grant reviews . . . then, an email response: "I can
help you."

By faith I sent an email back and a woman named Sherri Delmont responded immediately. Sherri, as I would learn, was a clinical nurse with access to a large database and considerable experience researching family connections. It was part of her job to find people; in fact, it was while conducting such a search that her email "looking for D. Wyatt" had shown up in my inbox. Coincidence? It was more like a clue from heaven itself, given that I had hit a barrier in my years-long search. The next day, Sherri and I talked. Through that impersonal email exchange, a wonderful friendship formed. Finally, perhaps miraculously, I had been given a friend who was willing to walk alongside me in what had thus far been a very solitary process.

Over the course of a few weeks and several conversations, I shared the identifying information file with her. We discovered our similarities—she also has three kids and works in the nonprofit sector—and our shared passion for helping others. We discussed HIV and the toll it had taken not only on my life but also my children's lives. We talked about the possibility of rejection by my birth mother and discussed my strained relationship with my adoptive mother. Rejection sucks!

My adoptive mother had taught me the valuable, often painful lesson of rejection. Her lesson was that not everyone would think highly of me, and the possibility of my birth mother's rejection could be just as real as my adoptive mother's had been. Sherri and I processed what finding my mother would mean to my children and my health. I dealt with the fact that, regardless of the outcome, what I was about to do would change my life forever. After the conversation had ended I sat with thoughts of rejection. Standing before the rear-view mirror of my life, I allowed myself to feel the lifelong sting, preparing my heart.

Sherri worked magic. It was late summer when she telephoned to give me a phone number. She explained that the number belonged to my mother Angela's sister, Percella, my aunt. Three days passed before I found the courage to pick up the phone. On a quiet Sunday evening I called.

"Hello Percella, I know you don't know me but my name is Catherine and I am looking for my biological mother." Understandably, the woman on the other end of the phone began to question me.

"Who is this? Who did you say you are?"

I told her my adoption file had been opened and had listed Angela as my mother. I also told her I understood she was Angela's sister and that this was the number I had been given. She began to inquire about my father. I told her the papers listed a James Freeman as my father.

She giggled and said, "Oh, is that so?" She became rude, almost angry. I apologized and said I was only looking for my mother and that if she could not help, we could just cut the conversation. She again began speaking rudely, so I hung up. She called back immediately. I answered, and this time she changed her attitude, asking more questions. I began listing her family's names, birthdates and information, things she could identify as true and authentic.

"Now tell me again, who you are." Once more I repeated my name. Again it seemed to enrage her. Again I hung up. She called back immediately. I did not answer this time. My heart sank. Disappointment surrounded me. I sat alone, rocking back and forth, unable to think about what I might do next. *Should I call Sherri? Should I drop it? Should I call Percella back?* I wondered. Then the phone rang. I didn't recognize the number from the caller ID and knew it wasn't Percella's number. I stared at the phone, and then answered it. It was Angela.

Speaking in a calm voice, she said, "Hello, Catherine, this is Angela. I understand you are looking for me. I am your mother." I was sitting on my deck hovering over a cup of tea, breathing deeply. I recall feeling excited and overwhelmingly happy to finally hear my birth mother's voice—her voice, a beautiful sound I'd heard only in my soul. Although her voice was music to my ears, I also felt apprehension. What if . . . ?

Another person was on the line—my sister Donna. "Hello, Catherine, I'm your little sister."

"Oh my God, I have a sister," I said.

"You have *two* sisters," I heard Angela's voice say.

"Hello, Catherine, I'm Diane," spoke another voice on the line.

"After I learned you were looking for me, I had to tell Diane and Donna first." Understanding, I asked, "Were you surprised?"

"Yes," they both said in unison.

"They were surprised to know they have an older sister." In a mature-sounding voice that was calm and reassuring, Angela continued, "My sister Percella called me to tell me you contacted her."

"Yes, I did. She was rude. So I hung up on her, twice."

Donna chimed in, "Yeah, she's something, alright. I'm not surprised."

My little sister's voice was so inviting, so curious. I knew right away we would be sisters.

Then Angela said, "Catherine, I need to tell you the truth. You don't have all the facts." The next two-and-a-half-hour conversation with Angela and my sisters changed my thinking in regard to the idea of family and what I had anticipated for so long. I was unprepared, to put it mildly, for what was to come.

"The adoption file you have has given you the wrong information."

"What do you mean? What part of the information is wrong?" "Catherine, your father was my mother's husband—Broderick, my stepfather. He began raping me when I was seven. I remember it being awful. At first I didn't know what he was doing, just that I didn't like it and it made me feel uncomfortable."

"Oh my God," I blurted out, taken aback by her words.

"He stole my innocence. I suppressed my feelings for years. I dealt with it the only way I knew how. And that was to not deal with it at all. It was an unspoken subject," she said, speaking in an oddly emotionless tone of voice, as though disassociating herself from the words coming out of her own mouth. After pausing briefly, the fullness of her trauma seemed to grip her and a stream of memories she'd clearly kept locked away until now came crashing into our unbelieving ears.

"Looking back on it, he systematically, progressively and strategically stalked me from the beginning of his relationship with my mother. At first he began 'accidentally' brushing up against me, putting his body close enough to rub against me while watching my reactions, ready to defend himself. I was a shy, reserved child. He had spent time befriending me, cultivating a relationship, and introducing innocent play, which made me feel special, but his play became more confusing. "

Her momentary pause was broken as she said, "He would sometimes wrestle and roughhouse with me and my sister Violet. I was a shy child. It took me some time to warm up to him, but over time and with the promptings of my mother, I did. He liked to tickle me a lot, and would chase me around the house and catch me. I thought he was playing a game. I did not realize that while tickling me he was feeding off my giggles and laughter. All that play provided opportunities for him to touch me, initially in an appropriate manner." Her breathing seemed to accelerate as she went on, retracing the path that had led from her stepfather's seemingly sincere affection to unimaginable betrayal.

"I came to enjoy his attention and enthusiastically participated. My mother seemed happy and did not say anything about his behavior, so I thought it was okay. I had no idea he was testing me, checking my reactions to his every word, every movement, every touch. He was a master manipulator, managing his position so he would be accepted and I would feel safe with him." She took a deep breath and paused.

"Oh, Mom," a sister said.

Primed and evidently ready to process her mother's horrific childhood aloud, Angela single-mindedly continued her monologue, increasing her intensity as she spoke. "When I watched TV he would snuggle beside me under a blanket. It all seemed so normal. Things changed, though, from him cuddling with me under a blanket in front of the TV to privately fixing me with sexually charged looks that made me feel self-conscious. I didn't really know what those expressions meant at the time, but in my gut I knew something very strange was beginning to happen."

We three sisters listened to our mother's words with heaviness, rage, disgust and disbelief. "Oh my God," I said, "I don't understand how . . ." My mind reeling with these appalling new revelations, I stopped in mid-sentence searching for words as Angela quickly resumed her story, probably unaware I'd said anything at all.

"His inappropriate looks soon escalated to rude comments and confusing, off-color jokes, told to me when others were not around," Angela said, her voice suddenly turning girlish and scared for just an instant. "I was so young and didn't understand. . . . As an adult, I learned the word for it: he was expertly using *coercion* on me, making me feel as though I was somehow playing along with his perverted desires. At least, he had probably convinced himself of that, psychopath that he was." As she spoke I could hear my sisters' labored breathing. All this was news to them as well.

"Momma, you alright"? Donna asked softly.

"Yes, I'm okay. I want Catherine to know the truth. You girls should know the truth. Over the years, wondering in my heart if this day would ever come, I processed parts of this . . . but, I must admit, not all of it."

"But you don't have to talk about it now," I interjected. "I'm okay with just getting to know you and my sisters. We can talk about that later."

"No, I want to. It's time." She went on. In a shaky, low tone, she revealed even more graphic details of her abuse. "I remember one time he pretended to take me to the store and use the family car as a place to molest me, touching my legs and running his hands up my thighs, grabbing my underwear. He seemed to become excited as he forced his fingers in me."

Diane interrupted, "*Damn!* Okay, Momma, stop. We've heard enough."

"Yes, Angela, please stop. I don't want to cause you pain by bringing all this back up." I said.

"No, girls, listen. I would sit stone-faced in utter silence, shaking and frightened, with tears streaming down my young face. I knew what was coming. Instead of going to the store he would take me to one of the empty lots where he was building a house, throw me in the back seat and get on top of me. My ear-piercing screams went unanswered and my tears were silent. To shut me up he'd sometimes put his hand over my mouth or a dirty rag in my mouth to keep me quiet."

"Momma, how did you . . . ? Where the *hell* was Grandma"? Donna demanded.

"My mother thought it wonderful that her husband accepted her daughters. The fact that he paid special attention to me made her smile. I remember watching her smile at us as I died inside beneath that blanket on the couch. I guess she did not see his hands groping me and his mouth near mine. *I did not like it!*" she suddenly bellowed, her long-dormant anger rising for perhaps the first time in her life. "I wanted it to *stop*!"

Her voice now broken and vulnerable, she moaned, "I wanted my mother to make it stop. I wanted her to make him leave me alone. But she didn't. It was easy for him to find ways to be alone with me."

Her words shocked us. For the first time, more than five decades after it all happened, she talked about the atrocities of her childhood. It seemed the floodgates of her past had opened irreversibly and she had to get it out. It seemed therapeutic for her to tell her daughters. As she spoke, my sisters and I silently grieved for our mother. We grieved our mother's stolen childhood.

Angela began again. "It happened so much, girls, I began to disconnect from myself, splitting myself mentally and emotionally to retreat from the psychological and physical violence. I became introverted and I had tormenting nightmares. I was powerless. My mother, your grandmother, kept me isolated from schoolmates, insisting I come straight home on those rare occasions I was allowed to walk home. Most of the time she took me to school and picked me up. It seems she didn't want me to talk to anyone, for fear I might talk about what was happening to me.

"As a child I blamed myself because my mother would not help me. I wondered if she loved me and I felt enormous shame. I felt trapped with no way to stop him."

My sister said, "Momma, that doesn't make sense. How you gonna blame yourself?"

"Wait, wait, wait, *hold* it," I said firmly. "This was *not* your fault. You didn't ask for this. You can't blame yourself for his actions."

"Yes, but—" I cut her off. "But nothing. You were a fourteen-year-old child. You were not in control."

"No, Catherine, I was twelve when you were conceived.

"Wait, *what*? But the adoption file said you were fourteen."

"They lied. It's wrong. I was twelve years old when you were born. They didn't want the hospital or Catholic Charities to know my real age. They did everything they could to cover it up."

"Damn, how calculating," a sister said.

As I caught my breath, quietly, I murmured, "Heaven help me handle my mother's words." Every wonderful thing I had imagined about my biological mother was ripped away. I sat silently. I had no words. At that moment my thoughts turned to my daughter and my love for her.

Crying, Donna whispered, "I can't believe it. How could this happen, Momma? What the hell is wrong with our family?"

"I just longed for my mother's rescue."

"Lord, of *course* you did!" The words spurted from me now. "You wanted your mother to protect you. You deserved your mother's protection. I would have felt the same way."

"She was no help to me."

"I know I'm talking about your mother, my grandmother, a woman I never met, but she sounds useless. The fact that she allowed this to happen to her child is just unfathomable."

"I was so young, so naive, so confused." Angela paused and then said, "The man was a master of manipulation and secrets. In every sense I was traumatized into obedience. To survive, I froze, which was the very best I could do. I did not realize I was being controlled."

"How were you able to go to school?" Diane asked.

"I liked school and got good grades. School was my escape. I had a friend in my class that I ate lunch with every day but I never told her. Remember, girls, it was a different day back then. You didn't tell family business to anyone. Kids were seen and not heard."

"Ma, did you ever tell daddy about Grandpa?"

"No, absolutely not! I saw no reason to tell him, but your dad knew I didn't like him. I made that very clear and your father was okay with it. I think he thought it had to do with me being his stepdaughter."

I uttered, "I am so sorry this happened to you. In the many years of imagining my mother, my family, and dreaming about you, I never imagined this as the reason for my birth."

"Damn," Donna spat.

"Shut up, Donna," Diane said.

"Girls, stop. Let me speak." Silently I welcomed the interruption of their sister-squabbling. Sobbing, she said, "The man's voice was very scary to me and he let me know he was in control."

"Yeah, I remember his voice. It was scary to me, too." Donna said.

"He berated, intimated, and dominated me in that house. I remember having to endure horrific, unimaginable sexual torture. I desperately wanted to confide in my mother, but he threatened to do to Violet what he was doing to me. His abuse overwhelmed me and I could not *stand* the thought of him touching my younger sister."

My sister said, "This whole thing pisses me off. Why didn't you tell us about this a long time ago, Ma?"

"I'm telling you *now.*"

"Wow," I said, "Okay, let's stop. I am not sure I can take any more."

"No, listen, my life in that house was a scorching nightmare. I established clear mental boundaries between my two very different worlds. He, in my mind, became two separate people, daddy and monster. I was ill-equipped to do anything, which was exactly what he was counting on."

"As you talk about him I can't help but think about his blood running through my veins. What does that say about *me*? Damn," I said under my breath.

"He simply carried on with me as if all was normal. By doing that, he created in me a sense of disbelief about what was happening. Combined with my mental state, each sexual violation was like a dream to me."

"Okay, let's change the subject. Did your brothers and sisters know what was happening to you?" I inquired.

"Violet knew. And the rest of them found out after you were born."

"And she said nothing?"

"Violet knew our mother knew. But what could she do? She was a child too."

"He bought me and Violet things kids like, maintaining his fatherhood routine. Both of them were real good at covering things up, which made people believe everything in our family was 'normal.'"

I said, "Yeah, it seems your mother was as good as he was at controlling her home." Sarcastically, I blurted out, "Sounds as though she was a good and faithful wife."

Then Angela threw this out: "His raping me became commonplace—so much so that ultimately, he did not concern himself with being exposed. It did not matter if my mother knew. He did not give a damn. He lived by his arrogant principle that women are inferior and property to be owned and used for serving men's masculine needs, all of which were governed by his upbringing and sense of male superiority."

"What the hell kinda mother *was* she to put up with his shit? I am so glad I didn't meet her."

Pausing, Angela then went on. "He knew how to handle my mother, how to make her toe the line. He was in control and she gave in to any and every thing he wanted. He was obviously having sex with her, because she got pregnant every year for eight years. And when I had you she was pregnant with her tenth child."

"Yeah, that's what I read in the adoption file. What happened to that baby? There's only nine of you.

"I think she miscarried it. After you were born I remember experiencing a whole new level of trauma. Having you scared me to death. I didn't know a thing about having a baby. And since I didn't have anyone to talk to about it, I stuffed it. I stuffed having you . . . locking the whole thing away in a safe place where I didn't have    to remember it . . . remember *you*."

"Grandma didn't get pregnant again after that, one of the sisters said."    "No, she didn't." Her voice trailed off again. I wondered to myself if I'd made a mistake finding my mother. A long silence hung on the phone line. The four of us pondered the words that hung in the air.

Then I said, "So I guess it did not matter what he was doing to you. Your mother was weak and gave her body to him too."

"Oh, he was smart and knew she was not going anywhere. She could not afford to leave him. Intimidation kept all of us in line, including her. He was the breadwinner. He had the job. His wife had the babies. After all, back then that's what good, upstanding churchgoing Catholic wives did."

My sister said, "Yeah, the old-school thought was 'what goes on in the house, stays in the house.'"

"Hmm, seems like too much shit stayed in the house," the other sister said.

Angela said "Yes, including the years of brutality I suffered." While my mother lived in denial of the events taking place in our home, I would get a sick feeling whenever his actions triggered the separation of my two worlds. It's strange; one of my worlds was filled with school projects, homework, playing with Violet, caring for my other siblings, playing with my dolls, hop-scotch, double-dutch and jump rope. My other world was filled with torment, secrets, pain, and nightmares of the repeated sexual invasions of my stepfather. I'd wake up screaming 'Momma, Momma, where *are* you Momma?'

"As our Catholic family attended church regularly, and we kids were baptized, over the next five years he committed horrific sex acts on me, from age seven to twelve, anywhere, anytime, day or night. He raped me from age seven until I was twelve, when I had you. He raped me several more times after you were born."

"Stop," I said, "I can't listen to any more."

"Catherine, it happened so much, so often, when I think back on it I do not know how I survived."

"Oh, oh, my soul," I muttered. "Okay, wait, the adoption file listed a James as my father and stated that your parents were in downtown Flint shopping and you had me at home," I said.

"Part of that is true. They were in Detroit trying to find a place to put me so I could have you. They were looking to place me in a home for unwed girls. They were not shopping. James, my stepbrother, never touched me. He was a good person and treated me like a little sister."

"Catherine, tell us about *you*." Donna said, clearly ready to switch gears in this conversation. I was grateful.

I began to tell them about my childhood, my love of dance, my husband, our move to Tennessee and subsequent divorce, my HIV diagnosis and all its associated losses. Briefly I told them about growing up with my adoptive mother and how I always felt detached from her. Most importantly I told Angela all about her three grandchildren, describing them to her; mine are her oldest. In her comments and questions about them, I could hear the happiness return to her voice.

Then something occurred to me that once again darkened the mood of the conversation. "Hold on, let me wrap my brain around this. The adoption file says you and Violet are not his biological children, right?" I asked.

"Yes, that's right."

"So that means Percella, Pearlina, Broderick Jr., Gail, Evette, Randolph, and Sabella, are *his* biological children, right?"

"Yes, that's right."

"So that means Percella, Pearlina, Broderick Jr., Gail, Evette, Randolph, and Sabella are my sisters and brothers *and* uncles and aunts."

Angela said, "Yes, Catherine, they are your sisters and brothers and they are your aunts and uncles."

"How twisted is *that?* This just keeps getting sicker and sicker. I don't know him, but I *do* know he was a son of a bitch," I said.

## Broken Innocence

*O*n a Friday evening in early October of 2005 I
boarded a plane for Atlanta. This trip would be life-
defining for me. After exiting the small-engine craft from
the tarmac, I managed to find the entrance of the airport
but could not find my bags at baggage claim. After
returning to the lower level of the airport terminal, I saw
a woman coming towards me. She moved briskly and
with determination. As she came closer, she said,
"Catherine." I said, "Yes," and we began crying as we fell
into each other's arms in a long-awaited embrace. We
hugged for a long while and she rubbed my arms.
Pausing only to look at me, she again rubbed my arms.
Time stopped.

The normally bustling Atlanta terminal was
surprisingly, eerily empty. I was finally in the arms of my
mother. We stood in the terminal for a time—I'm not

sure how long—just touching each other. As Angela's past stared her in the face, my future stared back at me. The product of Angela's childhood incest stood in front of her.

The drive to her house was filled with anticipation. I'd previously visited such local attractions as Underground Atlanta at Five Points, World of Coca-Cola, Georgia Aquarium, CNN Studios, Buckhead, the Centers for Disease Control and Prevention, and many other ATL hot spots for leisure and entertainment, but this trip was different. Arriving at her home, I was given a brief tour. Her three-bedroom home was cozy and seemed to suit her. Her décor was bright, airy and uncluttered. The house felt warm and homey but it was also neat and orderly. It reminded me of my own house and my preference for order; in fact, I smiled to myself at the recognition of this natural similarity between us. As we entered her living room she showed me a chair which had belonged to Tawana Jo. It was one of few possessions she had of her mother's, as the rest had been divided among her siblings. As I studied the chair's contours, running my fingers lightly across its upholstery, the grandmother who had been as intangible as a ghost suddenly became an actual person to me.

As I stood staring at the chair, imagining her sitting in it, I wondered if she came to the nursery of the hospital to see me. Making a mental note, I told myself to ask Angela later. Recalling her neglect of Angela, I felt a wave of fury rise within me—a righteous rage that came from being the mother of a girl myself. I shook it off; I was not going to let it spoil this precious time with Angela.

As she prepared dinner, I asked if I could help do anything. "No, make yourself at home," she said. "I cooked before I came to the airport, I'm just warming everything up. It's almost ready." I stood just out of her view, watching her for a long moment. I studied the contours of her body, her face, her movements, her hands, her voice, her personality, her hair, her smile. I was trying to find myself in her.

I had begun settling into the guest room when I heard Diane, my sister, walk through the front door, saying "Momma." I came out of the guest room quickly and we immediately hugged as she told Angela, "Wow, she looks just like Aunt Percella." Angela nodded in agreement.

As the three of us prepared dinner the two of them told me about my sisters/brothers who are my uncles and aunts—California cousins, Atlanta cousins, and how this one is connected to that one, that one has four kids, that one has two kids, that one's kids has kids, that one is on drugs, that one got out of jail, that one is married, don't nobody know where that one is, and on and on. It was all a blur and a lot to take in, I realized.

During dinner I studied Diane, noticing her personality being very different from her mother's. I studied Angela's easy interactions with her daughter and Diane's matter-of-fact tone towards her mother. As Diane shared remembrances of her grandparents, it seemed she gained a clearer understanding of her mother's childhood pain. My sister and I discussed commonalities. She has three children. I have three children. Her second child's name is Erin; my second child's name is Aaron. Donna, the youngest, called several times that evening from her home in Los Angeles. "I'm jealous 'cause I'm not there," she would say with each call.

Diane soon left, leaving Angela and me alone to talk. We talked all about her home, her church, spirituality and faith, her job, her first husband—my sister's father—her impending retirement, and the love of her life—her second husband. She talked about moving to Atlanta many years ago and about my sisters' childhoods.

Sitting in her guest room that evening, I got to know her in a relaxed setting, much less stressful than those stunningly revealing first phone conversations. Angela handed me Broderick's obituary and talked more about his heartlessness. I was transported down Angela's own memory lane through her many photo albums. Eagerly describing the story behind each picture, she opened the windows of my understanding as generations of my heritage lay before me. Seeing pictures of her as a little girl reminded me of my own daughter at that age, putting into grim perspective how this child's body had endured Broderick's torture and Tawana Jo's careless neglect. Also, the pictures of her reminded me of the many times I longed for her.

In the stillness of her guest room, lying in bed surrounded by her things with the light of the moon shining through the blinds, I reflected on all of the events of the day. The sky was bright with stars that night in Atlanta. Needless to say, sleep escaped me. Too many thoughts flooded my mind.

Knowing for the first time in my life my biological mother was sleeping in the next room I thought of the ties that bind four generations of black women: Tawana Jo, Angela, Catherine and Jalyon. Looking at the rays of light, I tried to soften my heart towards Tawana Jo, I tried. I still had questions but there would be time for them later.

The next morning I asked Angela about her health. She told me she's not on any medication but that she took vitamin supplements and her health was good. After a light breakfast, Angela and I cleaned the kitchen, ran errands around Lithonia, went shopping at the Lenox Mall, and had lunch at one of the fast food restaurants. The day passed quickly, with each sister calling to find out what we were up to.

That evening Angela invited Sabella over to meet me. Sabella, my half-sister as well as my aunt, brought two of her children with her. Although I felt as if I were on display, it was nonetheless thrilling to meet family. We were tied together by blood yet we had no history. I felt caught between being part of the conversation and being the topic of conversation, but I wanted to get to know these people. While feeling mostly at ease in this potentially awkward situation, I was fully aware my presence among new family exposed Angela's long-concealed secret.

Again alone in the guest room that evening, I reviewed the faces and conversations of the family members I'd just met, but sleep found me. After breakfast the next morning, on the drive to the airport, I mustered up enough courage to ask if she knew whether Tawana Jo, my grandmother, bothered to come to the hospital nursery to see me.

"No."

"So you didn't see me any more either?"

"No."

It was an emotional and tear-filled ride for me. Pulling up to the curb at the Hartfield-Jackson airport she looked at me and said, "I'm sorry, Catherine." I had no words, no more questions.

Vowing to call when I got home, I stood close to Angela as she once again rubbed my arms, seemingly to make sure I was real. I searched her face looking for . . . I'm not sure what. Upon entering my home, I called Angela to let her know I had arrived safely. Eagerly, Aaron and Jalyon wanted to know every detail. I spent the next few hours describing my children's grandmother, providing blow-by-blow playback including the fact that I do not look like Angela, Diane or Donna.

A week later, during one of the many phone conversations Angela and I had following my visit, she continued to paint a horrific portrait of her life. Disputing most of the information in the adoption file, she always had another fact to add. Although I was now able to put a face, a body and more personal feelings with her voice, it all still seemed inconceivable and I found it difficult to process. Imagining a child enduring so much at the hands of her father boggled my mind.

I asked, "Wait—was your mother sexually abused when she was a child?" Before she spoke, I apologized for asking so many questions about her mother. "I have such a difficult time wrapping my brain around her." I explained.

"I don't know if she was molested as a child. She didn't talk about her childhood much. She was from the generation that didn't talk about such things. But, she did work with him to cover up what he was doing to me."

"Sounds like something happened to her," I responded, "or maybe she was just crazy. She definitely manipulated the situation." I was overcome by the nauseating realization that my grandmother was a participating accomplice, her fingerprints all over Broderick's sexual violations. It wouldn't be until later that I would come to understand how his immorality had penetrated not only my mother, but in fact, had passed through their bloodline into subsequent generations.

"She covered it up from Catholic Charities, the church, the court, the school, family, friends, everyone. She blamed James for raping me, but she knew her husband was sexually abusing me." Breathless, I tried to find air, but I couldn't breathe. I grabbed my chest. "Oh my God. How could she not *do* anything? I am a mother. My daughter is my world. I would do *anything* to protect her. I don't understand."

She went on to say, "My family didn't believe in counseling, so I had to push my feelings aside. Human survival, I guess, will make even a child find ways to cope." Unable to speak, we both remained silent. "Lord have mercy," was all I could say. Again, silence. Softly crying, she said, "Yes, Lord have mercy. I was a *child*." With that, I too began to weep.

"He was so *mean*, Catherine. He was consumed by evil. He was pure, unadulterated evil. He was motivated by evil. His inner core was evil. He was cruel. He was a *bastard*. He caused so much pain in my life. I'm not sure I can describe to you the destruction. I was so alone, so young, so scared. He didn't deny what he did to me because no one questioned him. He ran that house with an iron fist and everyone in it."

Her voice quivering now, she said, "All these years I suppressed it all. But now I have to tell you the truth. You deserve to know the truth. You deserve to know the truth," she kept saying.

"Do you think your mother was afraid of him?" I stammered.

"I don't know what she felt. I just know she didn't do anything."

"Do you think she had an opportunity to do something?"

"Oh, yes," Angela replied, an angry tone rising in her voice. "She could have done something."

I felt sick at my stomach listening to her unpack more details of my beginnings, recalling the many times her stepfather invaded her so violently. She recalled her childhood house in Flint. "It was a hell house. I hated it. For years I had nightmares, difficulty falling asleep.

Actually, I was *afraid* to fall asleep—afraid he'd come get me. I was afraid all the time. Your birth frightened me. Keeping you was not an option. I was told to keep quiet. They were determined to get rid of you, the evidence of his infidelity, brutality, and her willing participation, as quickly as possible."

As Angela spoke I could not fathom how her mother allowed her daughter to withstand such barbaric treatment, how she could choose to sleep night after night, year after year, with a man who committed such atrocities. How could she look at Angela and not see the pain in her eyes? *Why?* A primal, white-hot knot of pain formed in my chest as the reality dawned on me anew that this monster is my sperm donor.

"The adoption file says you didn't want to hold me when Mrs. Brown asked you."

"Yes, that's true. I was afraid. I was afraid of you. I think I was in shock."

Angela recounted to me the years of physical and mental abuse she endured even after I was born. She recalled Broderick's double life as a child rapist and a committed Catholic who insisted his wife and children attend Mass as he manipulated Angela in the madness of his unholy masquerade. She lived a cruel life under the hands of her stepfather as he belittled her, called her fat, stupid, and other horrible things that continued to beat on and destroy her already fragile self-esteem.

On a three-way call with Donna and me, Angela told the "white rice" and basement stories. "We ate so much white rice. I cooked *so* much rice. The kids ate rice just about every day. I hate rice to this day."

"Wow, Mom, so that's why you don't eat white rice," Donna said softly. "I never knew that."

Then Angela recalled the basement, described in great detail as "a corner of the basement," as though that one small spot constituted her entire memory of the stale area at the bottom of the house. Angela said she remembered going into the basement to look for a gift and her stepfather cornering her and assaulting her for the first time.

She paused, seeming to tap into a blur of associated recollections, and said, "I would beg him to let me go. He'd ignore me." Then, with trembling voice, she said, "It happened more than once in that basement." She even recalled the musty basement smell before briefly changing the subject.

The reality of her abuse washed over me. I am alive because an innocent child suffered horrifically. Suffering for years. Suffering silently. My heart went to that corner of that basement, to that violated child. I was there again, this time as an adult. Angela journeyed back to her stepfather's volatile temper, and his ability to conceal it completely when it suited him to do so.

"He fooled everyone. He manipulated everyone outside our home into thinking he was a generous and wonderful man. In private, he was a tyrant. He would intimidate me into going down to that basement." Tears choking Angela's voice, she said, "I had no control of the incest, the rapes, and I didn't even know I was pregnant. I had you at age twelve."

The repetition in her words suggested to me that her survival had been based in dissociating from her rational mind. She was now experiencing the reality of her abuse in a part of herself she'd locked away. As I listened, she became that frightened child, again recalling the nightmare I'd brought back to her so abruptly. Just as quickly, she would regain her composure as the adult Angela returned speaking with great poise and dignity.

"It was not my fault. I was just a child. My mother knew. I know she did."

"Of course it was not your fault. You can't wear their guilt. The burden is too heavy." I sobbed as I listened to Angela longing for her mother's support all those years ago. I felt her pain as I had longed for that same love, and acceptance.

"Tell me about his family." I said. I wanted to find some understanding in her words. There had to be some information that wasn't steeped in abuse and horror.

"He was Creole, from Louisiana, and spoke fluent French. He came from a big family. Some of his siblings moved to Michigan and New York." Angela explained that he had died in 1994, there in Atlanta. "People had begun talking about 'the baby'," she said.

"You mean *me*?" I said, perhaps subconsciously refusing to be reduced any longer to an "it," as the adoption files had so liberally done.

"Yes, you. I think my mother was ashamed but she wouldn't admit it. She couldn't take the tongue lashings and whispers behind her back. So, one day she abruptly announced to all us kids that we were moving because she wanted to offer us a better life than Flint could provide."

Flint, her mother had told them, was a manufacturing, car-building town, and she wanted more than "shop jobs" for her family. Suddenly, as a mother myself, I was flooded with questions.

"How could your mother turn a blind eye? Why did she allow such an atrocity to occur, and do nothing?" catching my breath, I went on, "How could she do that to you? What the hell was she thinking? What kind of mother was she?" Under my breath I said, "Why would she allow this?"

"How could she lay next to, and have sex with, a man who was raping her daughter?" I said, feeling my emotions escalate in tandem with the pitch of my voice. Breathless, I went on. "How could she have sex with him and have his babies knowing he was violating you repeatedly? I can't wrap my brain around that," I said softly, searchingly. "As a mother, I just can't understand her."

"I don't understand it either," Angela said. "It was hard on me."

My heart melted as she spoke. As my questions poured out I felt myself getting angry again.

"Did he try to touch you after you moved to California?"

"Oh yes, he tried after you were born, *before* we moved."

"*What?*" I replied, incredulous.

"Oh yeah, he was a monster. By the time we moved to California I was thirteen, and I could and did fight him. Violet would fight him with me." I listened sympathetically as she shared some insight into how she lived through the abuse. "I hid shame, fear, and guilt," she said. "I had to learn how to deal with it where no one else could see. I coped with my feelings by being good, by getting good grades, taking care of my brothers and sisters, but the feelings were always there.

Even when things seemed to appear "normal", a simple trigger—smelling his cologne, seeing his shoes—would give me a flashback, sending me right back to when and where all the fears began: that basement. He destroyed my childhood. My mother destroyed my childhood. Sex was the furthest thing from my mind. I loved school, and being the oldest, my hands were full caring for all of them.

"I hated the idea of moving to L.A.," Angela said, "But after being there for a while I learned to adjust to it. While we lived in L.A.," she continued, "he made lots of money building apartment buildings and houses. But we, all of us, worked. We ate white rice and worked. He used us as his child labor. We all had to help, and that was that. As his two sons got older he used his manipulative prowess to intimidate them, forcing them to help with the family business after school and on weekends."

## Full Circle

"*W*hat about your mother? Did she like L.A.? What was she doing?" I wondered aloud.

"Momma was different after we moved. I couldn't tell how, but I knew she was. She was in charge of the checkbook and enjoyed spending his money. She lavished herself with furs and expensive clothes. She loved to dress up." Pausing, she then said, "Years passed, and when I was eighteen, I got a job, and left home. A few years later I met my first husband got married, had two kids and tried to forget. About seven years into the marriage, it ended."

"Did she give you any money?" I asked.

"No, and I didn't ask for any," answered Angela. "She bought my siblings expensive clothes and really did things big. Vacations and holidays were her opportunity to spend, spend, spend, and she did."

A few years later I met Sam. He was a good man. We married and a few years later the four of us moved to Atlanta. Your sisters loved Atlanta, and I wanted to escape the past, start over and get the hell away from L.A." As I listened to her, her voice sounded strained. "We don't have to talk about this anymore," I said. I wanted to relieve her of her memories.

"I'm okay," she uttered. "I was glad to be away from everyone. My husband and I got jobs, the girls had settled in and we were doing well. My mother came to visit us in Atlanta and bought a big house. She liked Atlanta and decided to move here."

"Wow, how did you feel about that?"

"There wasn't anything I could do about it, and she certainly didn't ask my opinion."

"What about *him*?" I asked. I listened intently as Angela went on. "Well, by then, Momma had made some lucrative investments. Broderick was sickly and had retired. He was old and acted like he was blind. Momma moved him into the Atlanta house. Sabella was on drugs in L.A., so Momma brought her kids with her to Atlanta to raise them."

"Sounds like your mother was in charge," I observed.

"Yep, she was. He spent the last years of his life in a dimly-lit basement bedroom while the rest of the family lived above him, ignoring his cries for companionship."

"What about your mother?"

"She left him in the basement, seldom going down to see him. She hired a nurse to come in to care for his needs. She saw to it that he was fed but found little reason to comfort him beyond that. He died a lingering death and was very much alone at the end. Momma seemed to exact her revenge from that. Her ignoring him became commonplace as we all followed her lead."

"How poetic," I said. I heard myself ask, "Was there anything good about him?" Angela said,

"He was a good carpenter. But even that caused great tension in the family." A silence fell, and then she said, "Catherine, I'm sorry. He was not a good man."

In my heart I prayed silently, *Father in heaven help me, help me to accept the words from the woman who bore me. God have mercy!* Refusing to refer to Broderick as my "father," I spoke of him as "him"—no name, just "him."

I questioned, "Was he an alcoholic?"

"No, he was not. He was a son of a bitch."

"And what was your mother?" I asked. Angela became quiet.

As I pondered our many conversations, I heard myself say out loud, "*I Am the Product of Rape.*"

"Yes, yes, Catherine, you are."

Finding Angela was not at all what I had hoped it would be. Never could I conceive in all those years of wondering about my origins that a man somewhere had committed such brutal acts of incest, raping a child who ultimately bore me. Never as I entertained my daydream wonderings—*Do I look like my mother? Does she remember my birthday? Is she thinking of me right now?*—could I have seen the brutality that resulted in my creation. The realization rendered me speechless. I cried, I cried and I cried some more.

After a period of deathly silence, Angela said, "Catherine, it's not your fault. It has been important to me that you know the truth."

As she spoke, I was transported back to that baby lying on the dirty floor of a stench-filled basement. The thought of it was all-consuming. *Oh, my God, my mother was raped! A child raped! A child having a child. And that child is me. I Am the Product of Rape. Frankly, I Am the Product of Incest!*

## Dirty Little Secret

*I*n the beginning of building a relationship living

less than three hundred miles apart, Angela, my sisters, their children, my children and I spent holidays and vacations together, even traveling to Hawaii. Meeting my biological family, having a family history, however horrific, was life-defining. Although intrigued and truly willing to know my birth mother, as I got to know her better through visits and frequent phone conversations my desire to tether myself to her had begun to diminish. A still, small voice inside me whispered continually, reminding me to be cautious.

In spite of the fact that we look nothing alike, I adore my sisters—especially Donna. Ten years my junior, she is a younger version of me, but much more bubbly. She is vibrant, always on the go and living the fast-paced

Los Angeles lifestyle. The time zone difference doesn't stop her or me from texting, which is mostly how we communicate.

The older of the two, Diane, has a more reserved, matter-of-fact, no-nonsense personality. Although welcoming of my place in the family, she remains standoffish. I enjoy watching the two of them interact. They are polar opposites and argue lovingly, but clearly they have a history together that I do not share. Often (even while in the same room), I found myself observing them from a distance.

Over the four-year lifespan of my relationship with my birth mother, Angela poured her heart into detailing her mother's little-known back story and honestly sharing the hard-to-hear, gruesome childhood details that led up to my grossly premature conception and resulted in my birth. She spent countless hours talking, remembering and answering every conceivable question I could pose, always saying, "Catherine, it's not your fault." I came to understand just how difficult it must have been to dredge up the past and talk about the impact her parents' actions had made on her life. But while our delicate relationship developed I began feeling a cautious uneasiness, especially when we were together.

On a Saturday morning in the late summer of 2008, I called Angela. She brought me up to date on the sale of her house, her plans to leave Lithonia, Ga., and her anticipation of moving in with Diane. House-hunting, the garage sale she had planned, her dread of downsizing, and her retirement plans were keeping her busy.

During that conversation she said, "When I let myself think about what happened to me, I mourn my life and I get mad at him and my mother and I still feel so powerless, even today. I was a happy child before my mother married that man. Then everything changed. My mother changed, too. The first time he, he . . . well, I don't have any more words to describe the dehumanizing horror of my childhood. It will never be possible to explain how this has affected me, Catherine. When I think back to the fact that I had to live in constant agony, breathe the same air as him, it sickens me."

I said firmly, "Although I understand this has to be difficult for you, I believe you still have an endless misery in your soul that is intertwined in my birth."

"Yes," she responded.

So, with enormous difficulty I learned that the man who deprived my birth mother of her innocence, mutilated her mind, and stole the most vulnerable years of her life was an incestuous rapist—*and* my father. I learned of a grandmother who, only on her deathbed, dying of breast cancer, apologized to her daughter for her role in the calculated brutality. I learned that Angela had told no one ever and had not begun to heal. I learned that my mother had two very different daughters and I discovered many twists, including the bizarre fact that I have uncles and aunts who are, in fact, my brothers and sisters. I learned that one of those brothers/uncles went to jail for sexually abusing his biological daughter.

Based upon Angela's recollection, I learned that the priest of the church I grew up in had known my birth family, respected the secretly perverted man who, unbeknownst to him, had destroyed Angela's life, and had been instrumental in my adoption. I also learned that Broderick's compulsive sexual appetite did not change after moving his family to Los Angeles. Upon leaving Flint in 1958, after working for General Motors for fifteen years, he became an entrepreneur, establishing the T&F Refurbishing Company. Using his children and stepchildren as child labor, he became known for exceptional construction in residential and commercial properties in and around South Central Los Angeles.

Unashamed and unrepentant of his sexual sins, his ghoulish nature was unstoppable. After the family relocated, his attacks on Angela continued, as did her mother's implicit acceptance of them, until she became old enough to fight back. Then his attention turned to women outside the Freeman home.

As I came to learn, one afternoon sometime in the mid-1960s Tawana Jo answered the door to find a young woman standing on the front steps. "Can I help you?" she said. The woman, who looked no more than eighteen years old, said, "My baby is your husband's child and I want some money." Unmoved but smiling, Tawana Jo looked at the young lady and said, "I'm sure it is." It was never made clear to me what happened to the young woman or the child after that day. But it would seem Tawana Jo's determined denial had hardened her heart.

As her children grew, so did her investments in land, property, furs and jewels, as she became accustomed to the wealth for which she'd sold her soul.

As my union with my mother progressed over time, trepidation mounted within my spirit. On a very cold Sunday evening in the winter of 2008, four years since first making contact, I was not surprised by Angela's call and what was to come. With the polite how-are-you's out of the way, her tone of voice different, the conversation took a left turn with her declaration "I can't do this anymore."

Calmly, I said, "You've painstakingly told me about him and Tawana Jo's treatment, but they're both dead. What does that have to do with me? I've met the sisters, brothers, nieces, nephews, cousins and your best friend in Los Angeles. So, what is this really about?"

"You," she said, "bring a lot of pain to the surface for me. I do not want to explain your existence to my church family, co-workers and everyone else who knows me."

"Oh, I get it; it's about having to explain a rape-conceived adult who happens to be your child."

"No one in Georgia knows about my past," she informed me, "And that is the way I want to keep it. I do not want to see you anymore. Your presence in my life causes me . . ." Her words faltered into silence. Then, finally, "It's not your fault, Catherine." Even though a relationship of sorts had developed, I did not allow her words to penetrate me.

I realized I was Angela's *dirty little secret.* Her image, the questions people would have and what people would say about her, and about me, became more important than our relationship. Deep within, I was not surprised. From the moment Sherri and I began this venture I had prepared my heart for the likelihood of being rejected by her or other family members.

As I spent time with Angela, interacting with her, watching her interactions with others, I studied her. Watching her body language, searching for clues, listening to what she would say, I became keenly aware over those four years of what she wasn't saying. During those years opinions formed in my mind, but I kept them to myself.

Life, betrayed relationships with those closest to me—my adopted mother, my husband—and common sense taught me to safeguard my heart. Even my nonprofit work in counseling and mentoring survivors of rape and sexual abuse and women with HIV/AIDS, sexually transmitted diseases and domestic violence trauma had helped to prepare me. Hell, life itself had prepared me.

She would not admit it, but I believed the truth was that whenever Angela looked at me, in her mind's eye she saw Broderick looking back at her. My very existence had become a lightning-rod reminder of rape. With the reemergence of pain my existence caused, she could no longer face the reality of her past. *I am her reality!* Another glaring fact to me was that she had not dealt with her pain at all and by no means had she begun the healing process.

Furthermore, I believed my biological mother remained stuck in her childhood pain, still mourning, still ashamed and, I think, still very angry. She chose not to take any opportunities along her life's journey to work through the trauma and begin the healing process. Because the two perpetrators of her torment are dead, I am the only reminder left to cause her anguish and take her resentment out on. Though *I Am the Product of Rape*, rape does not define me. I am Catherine!

Fortified by the grace of God's presence in my life, during that Sunday evening conversation I was empowered to tell her, "I am unwilling to allow your childhood pain-turned-adult-denial to dictate my worth. I've come too far, been through too much, to give you that much power. Listening to your many stories over the past four years, I have come to recognize that the child I was born to, even now as a woman, is not the judge of my personal value."

Making myself clear, I announced, "You have gifted me with missing parts of my life for which I am grateful. However, rather than addressing the many complex issues of your mother's capacity to use her daughter as a commodity, accepting of her husband's continued molestation which robbed you of your childhood, you have literally allowed it to incapacitate you. I am sorry, but that's not my problem. "

"You're right; it's not your fault, Catherine."

"Oh, I know it's not my fault. A relationship with you comes with conditions, conditions I am unwilling to accept. I have listened tirelessly to you tell me about the generational atrocities of your past, your truth. Though painful, it's your past, not mine."

"I know."

Before the conversation ended I had to tell her, "I refuse to be reduced to 'it.'"

Aside from the horrific treatment she endured, resulting in my birth on a dirty basement floor, I was not going to let that which Tawana Jo inflicted upon Angela be passed down to me. Her stepfather's immoral, inhumane violations and her mother's failure to rescue her had crippled her with regret, guilt, and many, many years of comfortable denial. Broderick, from the grave, was still allowed to exercise power and control over her. While I am Angela's biological daughter, I was not equipped to heal, to rescue, fix, or somehow repair her past pain. I understood that her wrongly-placed pain, projected on me, was not actually about me at all but was part of her unfinished business: the healing and forgiveness she had yet to work through. I was determined to reject Angela's rejection, finding fulfillment in the landscape of my life's destiny. Her truth actually set me free, giving me profound purpose, placing me on a path of self-worth.

I had entered into this search seeking the mother I so desperately longed for to fill an emptiness and provide a mother's love I had not known. However, during that search and after finding my biological mother and family, resulting in new relationships, I found something within my life's narrative I did not realize I had. I discovered I did not require a mother's love to define me and, factually, I had survived without it all along.

In retrospect, on that cold Sunday evening I had a full-circle moment. In my heart, my pursuit of an idealistic, happily-ever-after mother relationship ended, not in the arms of my adoring birth mother as I had anticipated, but at the foot of the Cross. For this, I will always be grateful to Angela. As an adult adoptee, the search for my mother's love and approval from a wellspring she was unable to access now defies logic. I am stronger for having had the journey!

## Who Is Catherine?

*P*art of knowing who I am is knowing where I came from. Under adverse circumstances, I was born underground to a naive twelve-year-old child among discarded rubbish on a filthy, disgusting basement floor. From that basement I was taken to St. Joseph Hospital. From there a nun took me to a Catholic church to be baptized and given a name, after which I was dropped off at an overcrowded foster home.

Thereafter I was shuffled through a foster care network that left me uncertain and unsettled. Over the next three years in the foster care system, bounced from one home to the next, the thing that resonates within me is this: from birth I was discarded, unwanted, unloved and homeless. Adopted by a woman whose heart had room for one child, I grew up living with a counterfeit story she told me to shut me up, which it did.

At such a fragile age, I had no roots. I was tossed back and forth between new foster placements like one of those discarded rags in that filthy basement. I have no memories of any other children in the homes where I was temporarily placed; however, my earliest memories are those of foster homes. I recall the fourth foster home in particular. Even after all these years I have vivid memories of a big white house with a long driveway that sat on a hill in a quiet neighborhood. The things I remember about the interior of the house are the rooms were neat and big, the walls were white, and it had a very long staircase.

Although I cannot see her face in my mind's eye, I recall a round-shaped female presence. Later I learned her name was Mrs. McClain. I also remember a red tricycle, which I loved. I have fond memories of riding up and down the sidewalk in front of that big house. Mrs. McClain would stand on the front porch and watch me, encouraging me with a big smile. Her smile covered her entire face.

Along the way someone gave me a doll. I named her Trudy. My best friend, confidant and constant companion, Trudy never left my side. Even then it was important to me that I keep her close. I still have her and keep her close today. Trudy knows all of my childhood pain and secrets. She has been my faithful friend over the decades and still holds that special place of lifelong companion in my heart. It's no wonder that I was so instantly drawn to the man who became my adopted father on the day we met. By repairing Trudy, he was showing love and concern for my only true friend, the most important entity in my life. Because he cared about her, I figured, he would be able to do the same for me.

Dance classes, starting at age three and continuing throughout high school and college, hold more than just pleasant memories. In retrospect, dance was my safe haven, my surrogate mother, my absolute lifeline. Dance became an indication of divine grace in my life. I was passionate about classical and jazz music, costumes and the theatre.

I loved movement through musical vibration, and my imagination would fill with the blissful, symphonic rhythms of craftsmen like Beethoven. As I grew older I was drawn to the talents of Tchaikovsky as the creativity of choreography became my passion. I found a strong sense of cultural identity in tap and modern jazz performances. By my mid-teens, my repertoire had advanced and I began teaching classes to younger students. I enjoyed costume design, lighting, makeup, hair, stage setting and attention to every detail. It all intrigued me, challenging me. Dance gave me dignity and grace in an environment where self-worth was scarce.

The art was hard work, requiring dedication a discipline that shaped my life's view. Through the challenges of dance, the twice-weekly participation in the art form, I gained confidence. Over time I was able to transfer that sense of accomplishment into the emptiness that followed me like a shadow—always there. In the music, and through movement and expression, I felt love. Oh yeah, you can bet I loved to get down to with street dance too and I had all the moves!

As an adult adoptee, I recall spending parts of my childhood imagining meeting and greeting my biological family members. Quickly, images would come into focus only to be interrupted by my reality. I found myself walking backwards in time, searching for that part of myself, imagining a "happy" biological family reunion. I was walking through the world, searching—searching for someone I resembled. I would look in wonderment at others with similar features to my own, and listen carefully when people would say, "You look just like. . . ."

This was especially true during my teen years, but I told no one of the emptiness I felt, except Trudy. Time and again I would picture having brothers and sisters, imagining that I was the oldest. Putting my active imagination to work, at bedtime I would tell Trudy stories about who I was, who I looked like, and where I came from. I recall telling her what it will be like to be the oldest, the smartest, the responsible one, and how great a big sister I would be.

For every joyous reunion I imagined, the possibility of rejection was always at the forefront of my thoughts. But any negative thought would soften as I imagined my mother's loving embrace. My process of searching for that elusive maternal unknown, which had begun only in my imagination, was mostly done with hopeful joy. Nevertheless, it was sometimes an arduous journey moving from simply imagining the day I would meet my real mother to actually undertaking the task.

Finding the courage to start the process was excruciating at times, and it took years. Believing in that long-imagined reunion meant having to fend off the fear of rejection that whispered its taunts of worthlessness to me. But at the core of my identity and ancestral pursuit was finding out the reason why I was given away for adoption.

Perhaps my desire to know my biological roots would not have been as intense if my adopted mother and I had made a meaningful connection. From the very beginning, she never took my feelings seriously. We shared moments of happiness, but, sadly, we could not find our way to a mother-daughter relationship.

As the years went by, the thought *I wonder if my mother remembers me?* would come and go, especially around my birthday. *Does she remember my birthday? What would my life be like if . . . ? What does she look like, and do I look like her? Would she even recognize me? Does she regret her decision?*

It was only in my early twenties, after I married and began having children, that I really became plugged into motherhood. My children's welcome presence in my life taught me the real meaning of limitless love. Their lives were always in the forefront of my every thought, decision, and action. From the moment I laid eyes on the beautiful face of my first child, born in 1981, to the incredible, unexpected miracle of my second child, born 368 days later in 1982, to the magical instant I was blessed with my third baby, a baldheaded little girl born in the summer of 1985, motherhood became more and more imbedded in me.

I was overjoyed with the birth of my third child, my first and only daughter. As I held her, rocked her, sang to her, and looked into her beautiful face, I had many thoughts about what it meant to be a mother, being able to share my biological heritage, knowing my bloodline and the meaning of family, not only for me but for my children as well. My infant daughter's smile, innocence, and laughter hardwired me into mothering a girl, unearthing primal instincts different from those I experienced with my sons. I loved all my children, equally, but having a daughter and giving her the kind of mother's love I never knew became critical to me.

I longed for my precious daughter to never feel what I had felt—loneliness, abandonment, alienation and confusion about who I was and where I'd come from. I needed her to have that which I had been denied: a mother's unconditional, unwavering, undeniable love. I wanted to be her strength when she felt weak, her calm in the storms of her life, her covering, her guide—her mother. It was essential to me to instill within her my love and wisdom, her generational identity, and the legacy of our past. As fulfilling as it was to hold a daughter in my arms, her presence seemed to highlight the absence of a mother in my own life.

As my love grew for my three babies, the undeniable desire to know my heritage began to grow within me in parallel. Finally, stirred to the brink of action by all the feelings parenthood had prompted in me, I decided to tell a friend about my long-held but unspoken desire to search for my biological mother. Her immediate comments took me by surprise. "Why would you want to find someone who has never cared for you?" she asked. "Don't you think she gave you up for a reason? Why do you have the need to bring more drama into your life? I don't understand your need to find someone who did not want you in the first place. Why would you even *think* about her? Girl, move on."

Her words burned me like hot ice. However, the hurting child inside me longed for *my* mother. Immediately, I understood, my friend could not comprehend my motivation to gain an understanding of my past. In response to my friend's blunt offerings, I said, "Finding my biological mother and family history is important to me. If you can't understand that, that's on you." I changed the subject.

Time passed. I got caught up in the business of life and, before I knew it, I was midway into my thirties. One day, my husband's parents asked me if I'd ever thought about looking for my biological mother. Outwardly I said "no" but in my heart I answered with a deepening and growing "yes." I said no because I wasn't ready to reveal the conversations that were going on within my mind and emotions. Tim, my husband, suggested that I think about it. I never told him this, but the thoughts never left me.

I resisted the pull because I knew that pursuing a search would upset Melinda. No matter how much she hurt me, she was the woman that raised me and I respected her for that. As far as she was concerned, she *was* my mother.

Nonetheless, her expressions of love were clearly limited to her favorite child and it was up to me to deal with that. I never told anyone outside our home, except Trudy, about the vast difference between the way she treated my brother and me. Outwardly all appeared fine; inwardly it was not. My self-esteem was extremely diminished. However, those years shaped me. I questioned everything, becoming self-determined, self-reliant, and emotionally independent while, in contrast, I found it difficult to attach to anyone.

As an adult, I have come to understand she could not give to me that which she did not have. Although my heart longed for a biological connection, the reality was that I was not her choice, and accepting that fact has taken a lifetime.

I have come to terms with both of the women who played the role of mother in my life. Both have taught me valuable lessons, the most significant one being this: the measure of my life is not found in my past or the circumstances by which I came to be. It is what I do with my life that matters!

## Epilogue
*By Jalyon Welsh-Cole*

## Burning House

    *I am Jalyon, the daughter of the Product of Rape and the fourth generation of women in my family to be touched by the violent acts of incest, which have roots in my family's bloodline. For two decades, I carried the burdensome pain alone. By the age of twenty-nine, the scales of secrecy had taken a tremendous toll on my emotional and psychological well-being. I could no longer keep the pain locked away because it was literally killing me. In a mentally unhealthy state, I decided it was time to unchain myself from the past, embrace inner peace, breathe, and allow myself to heal.*

    *Our family moved to Brentwood, Tennessee when I was five years old. My early childhood memories (age five through seven) are ones of great happiness. There were always a lot of activities in our home and a lot of kids in the neighborhood to play with. Being the youngest of three, and the only girl, allowed me a special place in my daddy's heart. He spoiled me, making me the center of the family, which was a* position I took seriously and held dearly. We were a close family, traveling often. My parents enjoyed taking us kids camping all over East Tennessee and other nearby places. We would go hiking along the trails at Fall Creek Falls, Natchez Trace, and other state parks.

Our adventurous family went hang-gliding over Red Top Mountain State Park, swam in its lakes, celebrated my seventh birthday with a huge Lion King-themed cake, ate dinner over a campfire, and slept in sleeping bags in our big blue family tent. We loved it when Mom would take us for long rides through the winding back country roads in her blue convertible dune buggy. We traveled to many parts of the country in our family van (which we called "our Bubba") with our potbelly pig on family vacations. A few weeks every summer, my parents, siblings, and I would visit my Grandmother Malinda in Michigan. Before life changed, our family went to San Francisco and Los Angeles to a family reunion. We spent a great day at Disneyland.

At home, I loved playing games and running around with my brothers. Although it was easy for me to make friends, I preferred hanging with my brothers instead. Any invitation to tag along with my brothers, although rare, I would eagerly accept. My big brothers were the coolest and most popular kids in our neighborhood. Being a girl never mattered because go-carts, kick ball, soccer, rollerblading, and street hockey always seemed so much more fun than typical girl-play.

Then nightfall would come. When the street lights came on, we had to be in the house. After a bath, I would climb into my two-piece pajama set and watch In

*Living Color. Then, like clockwork, Mom's voice would travel throughout the house, "Jalyon! Time for bed!"*

*Our four-story, eleven-room, four-car-garage, family home was located atop a breathtaking hill in an upscale, well-manicured Brentwood neighborhood at the end of a quiet cul-de-sac. The house was beautiful and our family was very happy there at first. We'd have nightly dinners, listening to jazz music with a lot of dinner-table talk and laughter.*

*I loved my bedroom. Mom decorated it in pink and purple wallpaper with pink trim. My bed cover and curtains had matching pink and purple lace borders. In the center of my bed was "Chubbs," my favorite companion. She and I connected the first moment I saw her. Her chubby, chocolate-colored plastic body captured my heart. I spent hours playing dress-up, dancing, and sharing my girlhood secrets with Chubbs. Mom hung a large net from the ceiling in a corner of my room. In it was every stuffed animal imaginable, big and small. I had collected them all during our family's travels, but none was as important to me as Chubbs.*

Chubbs

*My bedroom had a large walk-in closet where I kept a little red tea-time table with stuffed animals sitting in all four chairs. I spent countless hours at my pink makeup station, which had a small storage area that lifted into a* mirror where I kept "pretend" makeup. Everything an impressionable seven-year-old little girl could want was in my room. My family would say, "Your room stays messy," but that was how I liked it.

Next to my room was my brothers' shared room. Across from their room was one of three guest rooms. Jonathan, the oldest, was not the cleanest kid, which caused many problems between my brothers. As they got older, Aaron, the neat freak, asked to move into the guest room across the hall from Jonathan.

Mom, without explanation, was totally opposed to the idea of Aaron moving into the guest room. Dad thought it was a good idea for Aaron to have his own room, but Mom wasn't having it, turning him down every time he mentioned it to her. But with months of many heartfelt pleas, Aaron wore her down and finally convinced her to let him have his own room. Jonathan's room was next to mine and Aaron moved into the biggest room across the hall.

On a Sunday afternoon in early 1994, while sitting on the floor in my mother's bedroom at her feet, my world was rear-ended when she told me she and my dad were diagnosed with HIV, the virus that causes AIDS. As she spoke, I was consumed with fear. I didn't understand her explanation, so I asked if she was going to die. She tried to assure me that they both would be fine, but I knew better. I could tell my mother was trying to hold back her tears. As a young girl I knew this was only the beginning of something much deeper. Thinking I was too young, my parents had already told my brothers. It was only after my Mom was hospitalized that she decided I should know of her and *my father's illness. I became very afraid for my parents and our family's future.*

*Under the weight of HIV/AIDS, my family began changing, and the strain between my parents was apparent. Mom did not smile anymore. I remember seeing her with her head in her hands, as if she had too much on her mind. We stopped having family nights together. She tried to hide it, but she cried, a lot and often. Also, by then, my dad drank, a lot and often, hiding empty bottles around the house. Tension in the house was thick enough to cut with a knife. I thought my parents were dying and weren't telling me because they didn't want to worry me. But I was worried anyway. I loved my mom and dad. I loved my family and, as the center of it, I could feel it falling apart.*

*As the implosion of my family continued, Jonathan, no longer sharing a room, came into my room one night when everyone else was sleeping. He woke me up telling me to come get in bed with him. Sleepily, not thinking anything of it, and trusting him explicitly, I agreed and went with him. His bedroom walls were covered with posters of Metallica and Mega Death. His dirty clothes were scattered on his messy floor across the room and games spilled out into the floor. Climbing into his blue-painted, metal-framed twin-size bed in his messy room, he helped me in next to him, covering us both.*

*Snuggling next to my brother, we both fell asleep. Gullible, I thought nothing of falling asleep next to him. I felt safe knowing my brother would never hurt me, as the worry of our parents' impending death haunted my dreams.*

He would come into my room, wake me up and take me to his bed often, until (as I later came to realize) he was sure I felt safe with him. I was extremely vulnerable when my oldest brother began laying the groundwork for molesting and eventually raping me. I did not realize that I was watching the creation of a manipulative, domineering predator. My oldest brother had a slow, insidious evil undercurrent that simmered just beneath the surface --- one which very few people saw. My brothers having separate rooms became the beginning of my worst nightmare.

I was eight years old when, instead of covering us and going to sleep, Jonathan wanted to play under the covers. At first, I thought he was trying to tickle me and just playing around, as siblings often do. But his tickles turned to fondling, uncomfortable touching, licking, and groping. In succession, his advances grew more aggressive. On the first horrifying night, my brother not only sexually assaulted me, he pierced my very soul, altering the essence of my personality forever. Terrified, I gasped and cried, "NO, STOP, STOP!" but he covered my mouth, telling me "SHHH! Be quiet!" In shock, I laid there confused, bone-chillingly still, crying in silence because he was hurting me so badly. I didn't know what to do. I tried to get him off of me, but he was too heavy, and I could not push him off. He was much bigger and stronger than I was. I knew what he was doing felt so very, very wrong.

When he finished, he lifted the covers back and said sternly, "Go back to your bed." Stumbling to my room in excruciating pain, I climbed into my bed, hugged Chubbs, and cried myself to sleep with my face *in my pillow. Restless and frightened, that night I dreamed snakes were attacking me. They were everywhere: big ones, small ones, long ones, black ones, spotted ones, thousands of them coming at me, taunting me, hurting me. I woke up screaming. For many years to come, my dreams would be consumed by terrifying, angry snakes. The next morning he said nothing. I thought a lot about telling my mom, but I just couldn't. In retrospect, I was forever traumatized.*

*Several months passed, then he raped me again. This time, I felt warmth underneath me and a strong aroma of urine. He raped and urinated in me. I begged him to let me go, so I could change clothes. As he loosened his grip, I wiggled free and got out of his bed, sobbing, as I went into the bathroom to wash myself and change into clean pajamas.*

*The next morning, I prayed my mom would not notice I had on a different set of pajamas. I don't know why, but I feared if she noticed that I would be the one to get in trouble. I knew that wasn't true, but the fear still terrified me. So once again, I kept silent. As strange as it may sound, I felt as though my brother's repeated sexual assaults were somehow my fault, even though I knew differently and I knew what he was doing to me was wrong. After that, as I recall, I began biting my nails a lot. My mom would get on to me about it. Biting my nails became a nervous habit.*

*I trusted and loved my brother, but he trampled that trust by manipulating my innocence. For six hellish years, he invaded me many times, washing away my self-worth, self-respect, self-esteem, and shaping my outlook on men, relationships, and sex. Much bigger,*

*stronger, and four years my senior, his manipulation,
coercion, and control violated my youthful love in the
most abhorrent way. Sometimes, he would lure me into
his bedroom with tricks, bribes, or threats. Other times,
he would corner me in the basement, or the bathroom,
or the kitchen of our home, making overt statements
that set the tone for the night ahead. His words petrified
me, and I would dread the setting sun. He had become
my real-life boogeyman, but he wasn't under my bed.
He was very real. He lived in the next room — a living
nightmare for me. And, I didn't tell.*

*Time seemed to stand still, as my world buckled
beneath me in the summer of 1995, the day my dad
moved out. I feared this day, the day my family
foundation collapsed. Once my dad moved out, I knew
our lives would never be the same again.*

*During that time, my mother was sick often. It
wasn't out of character for my grandmother to come
and help take care of us when our parents were ill or
working extra hours. So, I asked mom if Grandma was
going to come down and take care of her. Mom told me
grandma was afraid of HIV. My young mind didn't
understand that because I didn't see HIV. I saw my
sick mother. I didn't understand why my grandmother
didn't want to see her sick daughter and how she could
suddenly stop coming to see us. To me, everything I
cared about was falling apart, and loss became my new
norm.*

*I desperately wanted to tell Mom, but I was lost
in paralyzing fear. If I were to tell her what my brother
had been doing to me, I knew something drastic would
happen. Though she was sick, had she known, without a*

doubt I knew she would not have allowed such a thing. That was the type of parent she was.

Mom made sure we had special time together. She called it "girl time." She'd take me to the nail salon and on dates out to eat. We'd have hair appointments and go shopping, showing me how fun being a girl was. I recall her picking me up from school early and taking me to Back Yard Burgers, our special place. I drooled over girl time and mom telling me how much she loved me. She'd call me her "best girlfriend," and she showed it.

She always put her children's well-being above her own. In my young mind, I imagined that if I told her that she would call the police and they would send him to a children's home, prison, juvenile detention, or even kill him. So I believed silence was my only option.

Throughout my adolescence, Mom talked to me about sex, my personal space, uncomfortable and inappropriate touching, and she told me to tell her if anyone ever touched me. She talked about getting my period and what to expect; when I started, she was prepared.

She would say she wanted me to know these things because her mother didn't tell her about getting her period, about boys, about uncomfortable touching, tampons versus pads, or overnight pads versus panty liners. She learned those things from other inexperienced girls, and that was not what she wanted for me. She wanted to be the kind of mother to me that she never had. That was extremely important to her, and she let me know it.

*Amidst the chaos surrounding us, to avoid being left alone with the sexual predator living in our home, I stayed close to Mom, literally clinging to her, as she tried to make life as normal as possible. In front of others, she put on a brave face, but, after Dad left, she was on her own, with no help from what little family or friends she had left. Little did she know, I was "pretending," too.*

*It was late 1997, and Mom and Dad had been divorced for about a year. I was twelve and was having trouble staying focused in school. I couldn't shake feelings of guilt, deep loneliness, and utter misery, and amidst it all, I missed my dad very much. My life had experienced so many losses, each one more devastating than the one before it, each altering my already very vulnerable world. Mom's brave face had faded under the pressure of Jonathan's toxic anger and uncontrollable physical violence toward Aaron and me. He didn't care that she was sick and, as a matter of fact, he took advantage of it by lying constantly and stealing money from her.*

*Taking advantage of any and every opportunity, he progressively became a brutal, insidious monster, sexually assaulting me frequently. His slow boil ignited, doubling-down into a full-blown inferno. One day, Jonathan threw me through a big plate glass window in our kitchen — no reason, just 'cause. On another occasion, he went into Aaron's room, took his pet hamster out of its tank and threw it out the bedroom window to the pavement below, as hard as he could, killing it — no reason, just 'cause.*

*Mom bought Aaron a black left-handed Ibanez bass guitar, amplifier and carrying case. He was so excited to learn how to play it. A friend from church began teaching him to play. Aaron loved his guitar so much. Jonathan stole it out of Aaron's bedroom and pawned it, leaving the amplifier and carrying case in the bedroom – no reason, just 'cause. Mom was pissed, but Aaron was devastated. When Aaron confronted Jonathan about the guitar, of course Jonathan denied it as he always did. With intense anger, Aaron looked into Jonathan's hijacked soul, as an unspoken something passed between them. Never would their relationship be the same.*

*No one had to do anything to light Jonathan's match. His match was always lit. He needed no reason; he was cruel. In order to survive the tornado my life had become, I was biting my nails so badly they would bleed.*

*In addition, I began separating my two very different worlds. My imagination created two worlds. One world was where I saw my tricky-wicked brother as a dark, heinous perpetrator, subjugating and demeaning me in every way. My other world, where my mom, dad, and Aaron were, was bright, loving and happy.*

*As I continued suppressing the hellish brutality I was living in, my childish mind learned the art of pretense in order to cope in my real-world hell. While I kept quiet, Mom took him to weekly psychiatrist sessions and got him in after-school tutoring three times a week, but he was not doing well in school. Meetings with principals, teachers, and tutors, parental* monitoring of his friends (he only had one), family counseling — nothing seemed to make a difference. None of the help she sought for him was working.

The high school guidance counselor recommended putting him in an all-male military boarding school. After researching several options, mom agreed, and the counselor found a scholarship to help her with his tuition, room and board. She did not realize that by taking Jonathan away she was actually saving me from the methodical perpetrator my brother had become. I was so happy and relieved he was gone, but I still could not tell her what he had done to me.

Pretending to be a well-adjusted adolescent became normal, but my young life was anything but normal. After losing her job, then our house, I later learned Mom was suffering financially. We moved to the mountains of Gatlinburg, where we lived for a year and a half. There my mother continued to write letters to us thinking her time on earth would be cut short due to HIV. Later, those letters would become her first book, "AIDS Memoir Journal of an HIV Positive Mother." Struggling emotionally with what our lives had become, I saw my mother drowning herself in her writings. She often said," There's so little time, but so much I need to tell you all. There's so much you need to know." Jonathan was still at boarding school. Mom would bring him home on holidays or long weekends, but mostly he lived at school. He did not touch me while we lived in Gatlinburg, because there were no opportunities.

In late summer of 1998, I had just turned thirteen when we moved back to Brentwood. When

*Jonathan was home he'd brag that he had joined a gang and that he had learned how to hurt people while he was in military school. He would tell me, "I know one hundred and one ways to kill you without anybody knowing." He terrified me. I remember one day, when Mom was at a meeting, Jonathan, who was sixteen at the time, barricaded me in my room saying he was going show me how easy it was to kill me. I was so scared. Screaming, I ran to the other side of my room and got under my bed, but he followed me and began suffocating me with my pillow while under my bed. Not knowing what was taking place, Aaron, then fifteen, hearing my muffled cries, came running upstairs and pulled Jonathan off of me, literally saving my life that day.*

*As that year progressed, he came home less frequently. I came to know my brother's inner core as pure satanic. His manipulative personality would sometimes switch to sweet, kind, even gentle, convincing those that didn't know his inner core. But I did. I knew, better than anyone, the fire that burned in him. Though the flame could smolder, I knew with just the right amount of wind, from the right direction, the fire could grow within seconds.*

*Fully aflame, Jonathan busted into my room startling me. Grabbing me from behind, he threw me onto my bed, and began raping me. All at once a voice called out, "Hey, guys," as my bedroom door flew open. It was Aaron. I recall thinking Aaron is here to save me again, but Jonathan didn't stop. As my body became numb to his brutal thrusts of pain, Aaron stood in the doorway frozen, in utter shock.*

Finally, someone else knew, and it gave me strength. Aaron, in sheer disbelief, did not say anything. As he turned away, I pushed Jonathan off, never saying a word. Composing myself, I looked for a long moment, deeply, into my oldest brother's hijacked soul, as an unspoken something passed between us. Then I walked out of my room. That unseen power came over me. I felt as if I had been given an internal super power. My new found self-power gave me the strength to stand up for myself and take control of my body. Jonathan never touched me again. At that point my physical and sexual hell stopped.

Two days later, he stopped going to school. Fed up with Jonathan's behavior, Mom was not going to allow him to live in her house and not go to school, so she put him out. She seemed exhausted by his constant disrespect of her, and his mistreatment of Aaron and me. She had had enough, but my mom had no idea.

At seventeen, a high school dropout, he called grandma, who sent him money, and he moved to Michigan. I was so glad he was gone. Finally, my tears put out the fire in my burning house, but my brother had scorched the earth beneath me in ways my teenage mind could not comprehend. The torture he had inflected upon me affected every aspect of my being, every aspect of life. I bore the scars and still told no one.

The backdrop of my adolescence was mostly spent being raped, sexually assaulted, and physically abused by my oldest brother. During the day, I took on the role of a young, carefree, mocha-colored little girl with pigtails. By fifth-grade, my life was coming unhinged. It was there that I was misdiagnosed with

*Attention-Deficit/Hyperactivity Disorder or ADHD,
but Mom adamantly disagreed with the diagnosis. My
comprehension, reading, visual processing and math
skills, with each year, became more difficult for me. I
was so broken inside. Focusing on school, homework, or
even friends was impossible at the time. However,
bringing home bad grades was unacceptable in our
house.*

*I smiled, but the hellish, traumatizing, snake-
filled nightmares, laced in visions of incest, drowned
my childhood and adolescence, plaguing my sleep.
Unable to tell anyone, I buried my pain deep within me,
unknowingly nurturing it, becoming a slave to it for
years. Time alone did not ease my suffering. Time
worsened it. Over those years of torment, I literally
developed a fear of being left alone.*

*As I grew older, the suppressed trauma of my
childhood had manifested, progressively taking severe
forms. I became more anxious, angry, and depressed.*

*I was angry that my brother repeatedly violated
me.*

*Angry my father had left.*

*Angry my mother was sick.*

*Angry because I could not control the things
that were happening to me.*

*And angry because I was angry in silence.*

*Hell, I was angry because I was angry.*

*Spiraling downward, entering high school, I
stopped caring about myself, losing all self-worth, self-
confidence, self-esteem, and self-respect. I became
challenged just getting out of bed in the morning, but I
couldn't sleep at night. I would cry for no reason. No*

matter how much I tried not to feel sad, it was like I was always alone, even in a crowd. It was difficult to just be me. I couldn't find me. I was stripped of who I really was.

Self-loathing prompted me toward sexual promiscuity, as a method of coping. Although I knew better, I managed to suppress my inner anger through the act of sex. Sex became an addiction, like a needle sending heroin straight into my vein.

The fact of the matter is, sex allowed me to manage life and subdue my pain. Nevertheless, as with any drug, it too began to let me down. Before realizing what was happening to my life, I had entered a lethal black hole in a downward spiral, leading toward the abyss of depression.

Just before I hit rock bottom, at eighteen, I became pregnant. Pregnancy enabled me to control my sexual dependency. Controlling myself meant having only one partner, my son's father. I skipped school, lied to my mother, lied to my friends, manipulated my anger management coach, and had friends lie for me, as an addict will do. I did this while still hiding the greatest pain of my life. I was truly suffering in silence. No matter how hard I tried to determine why I felt angry, depressed, or whatever feeling I was feeling at the time, I just could not figure out what was wrong with me.

A few years later my child's father and I separated and, instead of sex, my drug of choice became food. I felt like I could not escape the pain. No matter what drug I turned to, the residue of incest, repeated rape, molestation, and physical abuse were always *there. Like a shadow, each accompanied me, engulfing me, following me throughout my life.*

*At twenty-eight after suffering for so long, enduring so much misunderstood behavior, and questioning my own sanity, I was diagnosed with Bipolar Disorder I, Severe Depression, Anxiety Disorder, and Post Traumatic Stress Disorder (PTSD). My Mom was there during those dark days of diagnosis. The diagnosis made sense to me. It was then that my mother realized what I had been dealing with alone. She knew the pain I was in, but still she didn't know why.*

*Bipolar I had changed my personality. I had episodes ranging from extended periods of deep sadness and crying for no reason (depressed state) to impulsive hyperactive episodes of happiness (manic state). Then, once again, I would plummet toward the darkness of hopelessness, losing interest in activities that normally I enjoyed. At one point, while deeply depressed, I attempted suicide by cutting my wrist. Another time, I took a bottle of sleeping pills. Bipolar I had also changed my relationship with the one person, besides my child, I love the most — my mother.*

*A year later, one afternoon at the age of twenty-nine, in a manic state, I was in my office at Women On Maintaining Education and Nutrition, when I decided I was going to tell my mother. As I walked towards her office, I began to think that maybe I should wait, tell her at home; maybe I should tell her some other time, or maybe it will be too much for her. But as I approached her door I knew I could not keep up the pretense anymore.*

*Walking through her door, I was absolutely hysterical. The words "Mom, when I was eight, Jonathan began molesting me," fell out of my mouth like throw-up. Those words were the hardest I have ever said to her. Sitting at her desk, deeply engulfed in work, her jaw dropped. Her eyes widened. After I blurted it out, I immediately turned to walk out, and she shouted, "Wait a minute . . . WHAT? Where are you going?" I turned around, looked into her eyes, and saw my mother's soul begin to shatter. She said, "Oh no, you are not going to come in here and say that to me and walk out. You are going to come in here, sit down, and talk about it."*

*"No, Mom, I do not want to talk about it." I had not thought that far ahead. I had never thought, when I tell her, I am going to have to sit down and explain what took place. I didn't think I was going to have to relive it all over again. I just thought I needed to tell her. I was totally unprepared to unpack the whole sickening incest story but, of course, Mom insisted on knowing.*

*"No Jalyon, you are going to sit down, we are going to talk about it, right now."*

*"Okay, Mom."*

*I took a deep breath and said, "Jonathan was molesting me, raping me, hurting me. I couldn't tell you. I was scared. I know you, Mom — if I had told you, you would have done something. You would not have let it go."*

*"You're right, Jalyon, I would have done something. I would have stopped him. I would have*

helped you. I would have done whatever it took to help you. I can't believe you hid this for so long, daughter."

Nervously, stumbling over my words I said, "I know, Mom, but you did help me when you sent him away." As tears ran down my mother's face, I said, "Daddy was gone, and I was scared you were going to die of AIDS. So many of the people we knew were dying and I was scared I would lose you, too, and . . . I didn't want you to have that memory of me or him before you died." Catching my breath, I said, "Year after year went by, life happened, and I would have one more reason why I couldn't tell you."

I cried as I told my mother of the years of wicked torment, abuse, utter hell, and sheer terror I endured at the hands of my oldest brother. It all spilled out of me, like vomiting the bile of my past. She held me, listening patiently. I think she was more shocked than anything. I could tell by her reaction, by her facial expressions, she believed me. As I wept, she comforted me, telling me it was not my fault.

Utterly stunned, she sat listening to the gruesome acts perpetrated by the monster she'd given birth to, willing herself to stay calm. She didn't have the luxury of falling apart. She had to stay strong for me. She couldn't fix this like she could when I was little and fell down. There was no Band-Aid big enough to fix this one.

She insisted that I explain to her when the abuse began, how long it had persisted, and where she was when it was happening. I am sure learning what happened to me has wounded her beyond words, because I did not tell her what was happening at the *time. I can't imagine the pain it caused her to accept the fact that her son is a rapist. She was, and is, an amazing mom, undeserving of this cancerous wound.*

*Talking about it with her took me back in my mind to that place I have unsuccessfully struggled very hard to leave behind. There is absolutely nothing, nothing I can do. Nothing anyone can do to him will ever restore what he took from me.*

*My innocence cannot be restored.*
*My childhood cannot be changed.*
*My virginity cannot be restored.*
*My tears cannot be retracted.*
*My hurt cannot be stripped away nor repaired.*
*My scorched earth cannot be restored.*
*My nightmares and flashbacks are real.*

*My brother should have been a person whom I could trust. He should have been my protector. He should have saved me from harm. Instead he sought me out to intentionally harm me. He took advantage of our family. He betrayed my trust. He betrayed our mother's trust. He betrayed our family. He betrayed what we were taught as children. He betrayed himself. The demons he fought were inflicted upon me.*

*To this day, Jonathan has no idea of the trauma, torment, anguish, humiliation, and agony he inflicted by violating me. His actions are ground-zero leading directly to my Bipolar I diagnosis. He did not just rape me. He damaged my entire life's foundation in ways that he cannot begin to, and never will, understand. Hurting him in return will never equal what he has done. Ignoring and denying his actions are his go-to response. However, I was there. I am the one he violated. I remember. There is no running from myself or the truth.*

*Although these wounds will never dissipate, and while healing has its challenges, healing is possible. The first step toward healing for me was telling my mother. Talking to her was therapeutic. Incest, rape, molestation, and other forms of abuse can happen at the hands of a brother, uncle, grandfather, dad, boyfriend, trusted friend, or stranger.*

Catherine and Jalyon 1988

*Unbeknownst to me, incest, molestation, and rape are woven into the soundtrack of my bloodline. I faced the same systematic, progressive sexual domination, brutality, and humiliation my grandmother, Angela, suffered two generations prior.*

*She blamed herself for her predator's behavior and felt trapped, with no way to make him stop. I, too, carried that same cross, but I will no longer hide. It has taken a long, long, long time, but I will not live in shame. I choose to do something about it. I choose to take back my power! I am not my grandmother's shame. I am my mother's daughter!*

## My Bloodline Poem

*Before my birth the odds were already stacked against me. My future oozing the failures and sickness of those who came before me. You told the lies of happiness so well. Those lies follow me through the darkest shadows and are hinged to me. Even at my greatest point, I represent the filth that came before me. My lineage serenades like a broken record of grief and shame. The disgusting sins suppressed so many who came before the axe that sliced through the shadows. The pain you inflict stabs me and the blood that drips like death is the baseline of nature's current. The torment splitting me in half, forever changing my mental state of mind. Somehow the abuse is kept quiet to spare my loved ones the ache.*

*You were supposed to love me; you were supposed to save me from harm. Instead my innocence unknowingly taken before I could ever open my eyes. You beat my soul and shredded my future perception of men. The weight of our family chronicle suffocates me.*

*My mother's strength penetrates my skin and fills my lungs with air.*

*My mother guides my way, her strength lights my footprints. In her I see no signs of devastation, but she too is tainted by the foul bowel that is woven in our veins.*

*Somehow she sees the sunrise when our world is full of rain. She gently braced my flesh and pulled the muzzle from my face which restrained me.*

*She gave me courage to no longer live in silence.*
*I spoke my first words that day at age twenty-nine. At*
*conception my childhood already stolen, for I was still a*
*child. My mother held me like an infant swaddled in the*
*womb. Holding me closely and comforting me wrapped*
*inside her breast.*
*My mother gave me power.*
*My power gave me voice.*
*My voice gave me determination and my determination*
*fills the streets and land with purpose to do more.*
*Your revolting and wicked ways no longer chain me.*
*I did not ask to be born.*
*I did not ask to be violated.*
*I did not ask to be the girl who has to suffer in the*
*silence of pain my ancestors forcefully handed me.*
*You cannot have my power.*
*You cannot have my voice.*
*I have taken back what is rightfully mine. I will not be*
*silenced because you are ashamed and embarrassed of*
*what the world will see.*
*I will use my power to change lives.*
*I will use my voice to shout.*
*I will show you that your destruction stops with me*
*and will not taint my bloodline anymore. You are not*
*my secret. I wear my scars as badges as Jesus wears*
*His. Not as humiliation or disgrace.*
*I choose to do something about it.*
*I choose to take back my power!*
*I am not my grandmother's shame.*
        *I am my mother's daughter!*

*By Jalyon Welsh-Cole*

## Stopping Intergenerational Trauma

*O*ver the course of this often emotionally traumatizing pilgrimage, which exposed heartbreaking secrets, lies, immorality, and deceit, I found my truth. My original reasons for writing this book, which had to do with examining the cost of deception and deceit, expanded as I unearthed many of those hidden secrets.

Discovering that my life has been shrouded in *calculated* secrecy, deliberate deception, and resolute lies, I found a similarity Angela and I share. In finding her, I discovered Malinda had been less than truthful—frankly, painfully dishonest—when she told me my birth mother had said, "I told you, I don't want that damn baby. I don't want anything to do with it. Don't call me again."

The web of lies and omissions grew more complex and mind-boggling as I later learned Mrs. Brown (the neighbor who discovered Angela and me on the floor of the basement) is in fact Malinda's brother's wife (my aunt by adoption who I had known my entire life). Also, Malinda's brother, Mr. Brown, is listed as godfather on the baptismal record of one of my brothers/uncles. His wife, Mrs. Brown (my aunt) is named as godmother to one of my sisters/aunts, as well as being my godmother. My biological and adoptive families were actually connected in many ways. So many secrets, so much pain. For reasons known only to them, the graves of that generation hold many secrets.

Tragically, the consequences caused by Tawana Jo and Angela's silence created an unchecked intergenerational crisis contaminating my family's lineage. As my ancestors pass away with incestuous sexual impurity secrets, their *descendants* remain caught --- actually trapped --- in the carnage of abuse. However, rather than taking refuge in the silence of the two previous generations of women, I refuse to watch future generations suffer in silence. I did not know that my son was sexually abusing my daughter. I did not know of her pain. If I had known............... Although I cannot change her past, I can own the future.

Moving through this passage, it has become essential for me to stop the intergenerational trauma, historic oppression, and life-altering consequences that incest has cruelly and senselessly entrenched in my family. I recognize the past cannot be changed, but cycles *can* be broken, and future generations need not be bent by perversity in their ancestry. That starts with me. The testament of my past has been the transport used to propel me toward my purpose. Today, I have stopped searching for a mother's love and have found a purposeful, perfect love in Christ.

At the root of *I Am the Product of Rape—A Memoir* is "Burning House," my daughter's courageous truth. Often in her grueling endeavor she'd say, "I want to un-shame incest victims and bring awareness to others that even siblings can leave internal scars." Since the day she told me of the vile, contemptible secret that had burdened her for years, I have frequently searched myself, questioning myself as to why my son was so angry, searching my heart for answers, blaming myself for something I had done or said, as mothers so often do.

From the moment they were born, my three children had always been the center of my universe. I placed nothing, and no one, before them. Protecting them from harm has always been instinctual. I never imagined it would become necessary to protect my daughter from her brother and protect him from himself.

The old saying "all that is done in the dark eventually comes to light" is very true. Hindsight became 20/20 as Jalyon's confession of her brother's abuse brought our family history into crystal-clear perspective. Suddenly I understood his aloofness, his hostility towards his siblings, the deliberate distance he placed between himself and me, and his gasoline-filled temper, which would ignite into inexplicable rage.

It wasn't Jalyon. It wasn't Aaron. It wasn't me. It wasn't HIV/AIDS. It wasn't divorce. It was, it was . . . him. Somewhere along his life's path he allowed evil to take control of his character, stealing his heart and wiping away any human compassion. He became broken and vulnerable to the perverse spirits of his ancestors. Like his ancestors, he too kept secrets.

As her mother, as his mother, as the *Product of Rape* and from the shadows of our family history, I have had to face incestuous acts that were heinous and committed without remorse. Today, in search of healing, I lean not on my own understanding; instead, I fall at the feet of God and rest in His immeasurable grace, which enables me to endure this pain.

Having felt the malignancy of stigma, in addition to the wrath of rejection from others in my life, I was alone and thrust into single parenthood having lost everything and everyone. It was all I could do to keep a roof over my kids' heads. Under the best of circumstances, single parenthood, in and of itself, is not for wimps. For me it had become all-consuming, with each child taking me through different levels of parental *hell.* I had to learn how to be single, how to face life alone, how to face parenting alone, how to face severe financial drought, and how to face life with HIV/AIDS— alone.

With the intrusion of HIV/AIDS and the birth of W.O.M.E.N., I had begun to take on life's many challenges, believing HIV/AIDS prevention, education, treatment and care, as well as the fight against social stigma would be my sole purpose in life. Well, that's not the case. Guided by my personal relationship with Christ, my life's purpose has clearly deepened, becoming far greater than the one-pointed focus of HIV/AIDS and continuing with the lives this book will touch.

My hope is that this book will give voice to defenseless children --- those discarded at birth and the shy, quiet, traumatized children who have become introverted, silently suffering and living in the house with the monster of their nightmares. I hope it brings comfort to those who kept the secret and cried themselves to sleep each night. I pray it may somehow fortify the many that have been shuffled from foster home to foster home, as well as the many among them that became castaways, aging out of the foster care system only to face young adulthood emotionally unprepared and lacking the essential foundation of caring support. I hope it brings a strengthening sense of unity to those in search of (or perhaps who have found) their biological family only to be rejected a second time.

My desire is that this book will resonate with and safely liberate the unspoken truths of the woman who paints an impeccable smile on her face each day, a smile applied like flawless makeup, but which has become an unnatural and automatic grin distorted under the weight of shame-fueled secrets.

I pray this book will provide peace for the vulnerable woman who feels alone in a crowded room, shrouding her unspoken secret like the designer shoes that glove her feet. I also pray this book exposes the immorality of incest, rape, and sexual assault, and gives voice to those who have been sexually exploited, traded as a commodity (even within their own families), and used as property.

Offered in love, I hope *I Am the Product of Rape—A Memoir* brings comfort to those who need comforting. I hope it brings faith to those needing faith, and begins *Healing Secret Hurts.* Perhaps most of all, I hope it brings awareness to those in need of awareness and leads to liberating change for those who have lived in the bondage of abuse and secrecy, carrying that liberation into the generations still to come.

**HEALING FOR YOU**—Because you, precious reader, have taken the time to read this book, my daughter and I are compelled to offer healing solutions for those of you who have been touched by incest, rape, molestation, sexual assault, domestic violence, trauma, cover-up, foster care and the adoption process, all of which can have long-lasting effects. We placed Dealing With Healing at the end of the book because each of us is on our own personal journey towards healing. It is our purpose to use our life's experience as an example of healing. The process of healing is different for each person. You have read about the generational consequences of a woman's conscious decision to deny the evidence and allow her husband to sexually abuse her oldest daughter, a decision in the end, affecting generations of women she would never meet. Also shared, has been a twelve-year-old child's sexual assault by her stepfather, resulting in the birth and ultimate rejection of an innocent, yet unwanted child. You have read the gruesome truth of the fourth generation of our family affected by intergenerational trauma. Please take the time to think about healing. The items listed below could save, or at least change, your life. From the list below, ask yourself at what stage am I? Get help!

**What's the Deal?-** Should I tell anyone about the things I'm struggling with? Will anyone believe me, or understand? These are difficult and personal questions. No one can feel your pain. No one can feel your emotions. Only you can—and you have a right to feel what you feel. In time, you can embrace healing.

**Not Dealing-** I have pushed my pain away. I don't want to talk about it with anyone. I don't want anyone to judge me. I still have triggers. I feel guilty, I don't admit it, and I blame myself. In time, you can embrace healing.

**Dealing-** Love yourself. Be kind to yourself. Do not blame yourself. Do not give up on yourself. In time, you can embrace healing.

**Write My Deal-** Write it down. Get out of your head. Deal with your thoughts, pain, and anger. In time, you can embrace healing.

**Declare My Deal-** Take your inner power back. Own it. Say this out loud: I am worthy. I am strong. I am brave. I am powerful. In time, you can embrace healing.

**Defend My Deal-** Empower yourself. Take self-defense classes. In time, you can embrace healing.

**Therapeutic Dealing–** Your mental health is important. Open up and talk about it with someone safe. Listen to your heart. Say how you feel. In time, you can embrace healing.

**Day-to-Day Dealing–** Yes, I can do this. Every day I am stronger. My inner core is stronger. In time, you can embrace healing.

**Strength in Dealing–** Support groups can provide healing. Recognize you are not alone. In time, you can embrace healing.

**Holistic Dealing–** Close your eyes, take four slow deep breaths in through your nose and let them out through your mouth. Open your eyes and focus on what you're feeling in the present moment. In time, you can embrace healing.

**It's Your Turn to Deal–** You do not deserve what happened to you. You are not permanently damaged. You are worth healing. It is your time to heal!

**I Am Dealing–** I am beautiful. I am powerful. I am healing.

# Notes

## Resources

Centers for Disease Control and Prevention—
https://www.cdc.gov/violenceprevention

Centers for Disease Control and Prevention Publications—
https://www.cdc.gov/violenceprevention/sexualviolence/index.html

RAINN—
800.656.4673
National hotline, serving people affected by sexual violence. It automatically routes the caller to their nearest sexual assault service provider.

NSOPW—
https://www.nsopw.gov/en/Search/Verification
The only U.S. government website that links public state, territorial, and tribal sex offender registries from one national search site.

National Child Abuse Hotline—
1-800-422-4453
Provide local referrals for services. A centralized call center provides caller with the option of talking to a counselor. They are connected to a language line that can provide service in over 140 languages.

Network of Victim Assistance—
www.novabucks.org/otherinformation/incest

Justice For Children—
www.justiceforchildren.org

Catherine Wyatt-Morley—
www.CatherineWyattMorley.com
Women On Maintaining Education and Nutrition
www.educatingwomen.org
615-256-3882


National Suicide Prevention Lifeline—
www.suicidepreventionlifeline.org/
1-800-273-8255


National Center for Posttraumatic Stress Disorder, U.S.
Department of Veterans Affairs—
Phone: 800-273-8255

Childhelp National Child Abuse Hotline—
Phone Number: 800-4-A-CHILD (800-422-4453)

Depression and Bipolar Support Alliance—
Phone Number: 800-826-3632

Boys Town National Hotline—
Crisis hotline that helps parents and children cope with stress
and anxiety
Phone Number: 800-448-3000


Hopeline—
Phone Number: 800-442-HOPE (4673)

Rape, Abuse and Incest National Network Hotline—
www.rainn.org or (800) 656-HOPE


Mental Health America—
For a referral to specific mental health service or support
program in your community
Phone Number: 800-969-NMHA (6642)

*National Alliance on Mental Illness—*
*Provides support, information, and referrals*
*Phone Number: 800-950-NAMI (6264)*

*National Association of Anorexia Nervosa and Associated*
*Disorders—*
*Phone Number: 847-831-3438*

*National Center for Victims of Crime—*
*Multi-language service available*
*Phone Number: 800-FYI-CALL (394-2255)*

*National Domestic Violence Hotline—*
*Phone Number: 800-799-SAFE (7233)*
*Support services, help, and guidance to people struggling with*
*eating disorders, their loved ones, and families*
*Phone Number: 800-931-2237*

*National Runaway Switchboard—*
*Phone Number: 800-RUNAWAY (800-786-2929)*

*National Sexual Assault Hotline—*
*Phone Number: 800-656-HOPE (4673)*

*National Suicide Prevention Hotline—*
*Phone Number: 800-273-TALK (8255)*

*Office on Women's Health—*
*https://www.womenshealth.gov*
*OWH Helpline 1-800-994-9662*

*Postpartum Support International—*
*Phone Number: 800-994-4PPD (4773)*

*PPD Moms—*
*Phone Number: 800-PPD-MOMS (800-773-6667)*

*S.A.F.E. Alternatives—*
*Phone Number: 800-DONTCUT (800-366-8288)*